Financial Accounting
Issues and Cases

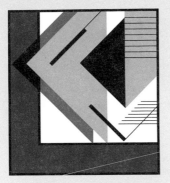

Financial Accounting
Issues and Cases

Michael C. Knapp
University of Oklahoma

West Publishing Company
Minneapolis/St. Paul • New York • Los Angeles • San Francisco

WEST'S COMMITMENT TO THE ENVIRONMENT

In 1906, West Publishing Company began recycling materials left over from the production of books. This began a tradition of efficient and responsible use of resources. Today, up to 95 percent of our legal books and 70 percent of our college and school texts are printed on recycled, acid-free stock. West also recycles nearly 22 million pounds of scrap paper annually—the equivalent of 181,717 trees. Since the 1960s, West has devised ways to capture and recycle waste inks, solvents, oils, and vapors created in the printing process. We also recycle plastics of all kinds, wood, glass, corrugated cardboard, and batteries, and have eliminated the use of styrofoam book packaging. We at West are proud of the longevity and the scope of our commitment to the environment.

Production, Prepress, Printing and Binding by West Publishing Company.

COPYRIGHT © 1994 by WEST PUBLISHING COMPANY
610 Opperman Drive
P.O. Box 64526
St. Paul, MN 55164–0526

Library of Congress Cataloging-in-Publication Data
Knapp, Michael Chris, 1954–
    Financial accounting: issues and cases / Michael C. Knapp.
    p. cm.
    Includes index.
    ISBN 0–314–02388–7 (soft)
    1. Accounting—Case studies. I. Title.
HF5635.K74 1993   93-3894
657—dc20   CIP

DEDICATION

To Bill and Orebel

CONTENTS

CASE 1.1   IN SEARCH OF PACIOLI   3

As the public accounting profession prepares to enter
the next century, it faces a number of problems that
threaten its credibility, if not viability. This case provides an overview of the evolution of accounting and
then discusses the challenges to which the public accounting profession must respond in the years to
come if it is to remain viable.

CASE 2.1   FLOWERS FOR ALL OCCASIONS   23

Florafax International, Inc., a public company in the
flowers-by-wire industry, overstated its reported earn-

ings by abusing the revenue recognition rules of the accounting profession.

Violations of the "matching principle" resulted in sanctions being imposed by the Securities and Exchange Commission on a company that owned and operated a large chain of disco dance clubs.

The accounting profession has faced mounting criticism in recent years for its approach to earnings measurement. This case examines the key issues central to this controversy and discusses methods for assessing the "quality" of accounting earnings figures.

The Video Station, a California-based company which pioneered the video rental industry, misrepresented its financial condition and operating results by failing to account properly for videotapes held for rental purposes and those held for sale.

The valuation of impaired assets and accounting for contingencies were major issues faced during the

1980s by a company which had a significant investment in a wind power development project.

Stauffer Chemical Company was criticized by the Securities and Exchange Commission for its unique method of applying the last-in, first-out (LIFO) method of accounting for inventory.

SECTION FOUR   FUNDAMENTAL CONCEPTS
OF ACCOUNTING   93

The adequacy and fairness of financial disclosure is a major concern of both the Securities and Exchange Commission and the Financial Accounting Standards Board. This case addresses important conceptual and implementation issues relating to the accounting profession's financial disclosure rules.

Possibly the oldest debate in the accounting profession centers on the question of whether historical costs or some version of current value should be used for balance sheet reporting purposes. In recent years, much of this debate has focused on the proper valuation basis to use for marketable securities.

This case discusses fundamental internal control concepts and then illustrates the problems that two organizations, E.F. Hutton & Company and the Los Angeles Dodgers professional baseball team, experienced when they suffered breakdowns in their internal control structures.

Irving Goldberg, an accountant employed by a large transportation company, was faced with an ethical dilemma when he was pressured by his superiors to misrepresent his company's operating results.

Following the severe financial crises experienced by the banking and savings and loan industries during the 1980s, public accounting firms were sued for billions of dollars by parties charging that these firms had been negligent in auditing financial institutions that eventually failed. This case explores three ethical dilemmas encountered by auditors of financial institutions during the 1980s.

PREFACE

Major changes are occurring presently in undergraduate and graduate accounting programs across the nation. These changes are largely in response to the growing perception that accounting curricula are not providing prospective accountants with the skills necessary to succeed in rapidly changing and increasingly complex work roles. Likewise, accounting educators have been criticized for failing to provide business majors outside the accounting field with a thorough understanding of fundamental accounting concepts, sufficient insight into the role of accounting in organizations, or an appreciation of the nature and importance of the various work roles in the accounting profession. The most common recommendation to overcome the present deficiencies in accounting curricula is to employ a broader array of instructional methods, particularly methods that are experiential in nature and designed to develop higher-order learning skills.

A primary objective of the Accounting Education Change Commission (AECC) is to encourage the development of innovative instructional materials for use in accounting courses. In its second position paper, the AECC focused specifically on the need for accounting educators to reevaluate the content and instructional approach of the introductory financial accounting course. In particular, the AECC encouraged instructors in that course to consider using cases, simulations, and group projects that involve active student participation rather than traditional, textbook-dependent methods that emphasize memorization of accounting rules and concepts.

The principal purpose of this casebook is to provide instructors in the introductory financial accounting course with case materials that will permit both accounting and nonaccounting majors to acquire a deeper, more integrated understanding of fundamental accounting concepts and issues. The AECC has suggested that students in introductory financial accounting should be introduced in a more meaningful way to topics such as ethical issues within the profession; evolving conceptual debates and controversies within the profession; key qualitative characteristics of accounting information; the role of accounting in satisfying the information needs of financial decision makers; the history of accounting; and the role and purpose of independent auditing. This text provides cases covering each of those topics as well as many others. For instance, two of the cases focus exclusively on ethical issues, while several others highlight ethical issues relating to accountants or the practice of accounting. Particular emphasis is placed on introducing students to controversial accounting issues such as the use of historical costs versus current values for balance sheet reporting purposes and the long-standing controversy regarding accounting's approach to income measurement. Other cases focus on important accounting issues or concepts related to a specific topic, such as internal control and inventory accounting.

All of the cases presented in this text document actual events or situations involving accountants. The names of the individuals and organizations involved in these cases have *not* been changed, the purpose being to promote the realism of the cases. The annotated Table of Contents provides a brief synopsis of each case to assist instructors in determining at which point to incorporate specific cases in their courses. Several of the cases can be integrated at practically any point in the introductory financial accounting course, for instance, the *Irving Goldberg, Corporate Accountant* case which highlights the ethical responsibilities of accountants in private practice and the *In Search of Pacioli* case which provides an overview of the evolution, societal role, and challenges presently facing the public accounting profession. Conversely, cases such as *Pools, Puddles, and Inventory Accounting* and *Insiders, Iniquity, and Internal Control* are best suited for coverage in conjunction with a specific topic in the introductory financial accounting course.

Although designed primarily for the introductory financial accounting course at the undergraduate level, the challenging nature of the cases in this casebook make it suitable as an ancillary text for a number of other accounting courses, including honors introductory financial accounting, the introductory financial accounting course included in most MBA programs, and the first intermediate accounting course.

To facilitate the use of the cases in a broad range of financial accounting courses, the questions appended to each case vary in type and degree of intensity. The first few questions for each case generally focus on specific technical issues, while subsequent questions are more conceptual and open-ended in nature. The final question for each case is project-oriented. Given the perceived need to develop the communication skills of accounting students and other business majors, many of the project-oriented questions involve a written assignment of some type. For instance, one such question requires students to assume the role of an accountant who must write a memorandum to his superiors regarding a critical mistake he has made, while another requires students to draft an appropriate financial statement footnote to explain revenue recognition decisions made for questionable sales transactions. Instructors in the introductory financial accounting course will likely find the focused, technical questions appropriate for the level of understanding expected of their students, while instructors in the more advanced courses will be inclined to assign the conceptual questions. The project-oriented questions, particularly those involving a written assignment, are designed to be suitable for a broad range of financial accounting courses.

The instructor's manual provides detailed guidance to instructors, particularly those who have never used cases before, on how to incorporate case materials in their financial accounting courses. The instructor's manual for each case includes a synopsis, a listing of key facts, a listing of instructional objectives, specific suggestions for classroom use, and suggested solutions to the case questions. In developing this casebook, the most common concern that I encountered from accounting instructors, particularly individuals who teach the introductory financial accounting course, was the lack of sufficient time to include additional materials in their courses. Certainly, this is a valid concern, but given the apparent need to enhance the learning experience afforded by accounting curricula, instructors should make every effort to incorporate innovative and experiential instructional materials in their courses. A primary intent of the instructor's manual is to help instructors minimize the amount of time required to integrate the cases into their courses. In this same vein, the customizing option discussed below offers instructors the opportunity to choose a subset of cases on topics which they consider particularly critical.

THE CUSTOMIZED CASEBOOK OPTION: WESTEXT ™

To maximize flexibility in using these cases, West Publishing Company has included *Financial Accounting: Issues and Cases* in its custom publishing program, Westext.™ This program makes it possible for adopters to create a customized casebook ideally suited for their needs. For more information on how to design your own customized casebook, please contact your West sales representative.

ACKNOWLEDGMENTS

I greatly appreciate the insight and suggestions provided by the following reviewers during the writing of this casebook: D'Arcy Becker, University of New Mexico; Edward Butts, Gray's Harbor College; Charles Christianson, Luther College; Roberta Marquette, University of Akron; Marcia Niles, University of Idaho; Sandra Scheuermann, University of Southwestern Louisiana; David Sinason, University of North Florida; Sammy Smith, Stephen F. Austin State University; S. Thiagarajan, Northwestern University; Mark Trombley, University of Arizona; Sterling Wetzel, Oklahoma State University; and Stephen Willits, Bucknell University. This project has also benefited greatly from the guidance and assistance of Rick Leyh and Jessica Evans of West Educational Publishing.

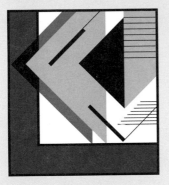

SECTION ONE

THE ACCOUNTING PROFESSION: PAST, PRESENT, AND FUTURE

Case 1.1   In Search of Pacioli

CASE 1.1
IN SEARCH OF PACIOLI

On November 10, 1494, Frater Lucas Bartolomes Pacioli, a Franciscan monk and mathematics scholar liv-
ing in present day Italy, published a lengthy book
with the imposing title of *Summa de Arithmetica Geom-
etria Proportioni et Proportionalita* which translates into
"Everything About Arithmetic, Geometry and Proportion." One section of Pacioli's text was entitled "De
Computis et Scripturis," or, in present day English,
"Of Reckonings and Writings." Brother Luke, as Pacioli was known by his closest friends and associates,
dedicated this section of his book to a prominent local
merchant since it described the mechanics of double-
entry bookkeeping. Pacioli included the bookkeeping
section in his text because he recognized the need for
merchants to have a standardized and easily imple-

mented system for recording business transactions. One of the first copies of Pacioli's text was reserved for his close friend, Leonardo da Vinci. A few years later, da Vinci and Pacioli would collaborate on another mathematics book, *Divina Proportione*.

Pacioli often referred to double-entry bookkeeping as the "method of Venice" since variations of this financial recordkeeping system had been in use for several decades in Venice. Although Pacioli did not invent or claim to invent double-entry bookkeeping, his 1494 text did formalize and document this method of recording business transactions; consequently, he is generally credited with being the founding father of modern day accounting. Following the publication of Pacioli's book, double-entry bookkeeping spread rapidly across Europe. The availability of a systematic and easy to use method of recording business transactions greatly facilitated commerce both within and between the countries of Europe, and, as a result, contributed significantly to the economic development of that important region of the world.

ACCOUNTING COMES TO THE U.S.

Since the time of Pacioli, the fundamental *rules* of double-entry bookkeeping have changed very little. However, accounting *practice* has undergone radical changes over that time, particularly during the twentieth century within the United States. As in most countries, accounting in the United States has evolved into two distinct sectors, private and public accounting. Accountants who work in the private sector are employed by one company or organization, while accountants employed by public accounting firms provide a variety of accounting and related services to the general public, including independent auditing, taxation services, bookkeeping, and a variety of consulting services. Historically, accounting in the United States has been dominated by public accounting firms, particularly the six large accounting firms collectively known as the Big Six.[1]

Public accounting was introduced to the United States principally by English and Scottish accountants retained by European companies that had invested heavily in commercial enterprises in the United States during the nineteenth century. Eventually, several of the largest English and Scottish accounting firms established permanent offices in the United States, one of the first being the prestigious firm of Price Waterhouse. The principal service provided by these firms was independent auditing. The economic self-interest of the management and owners of a company causes third parties to question the integrity of financial statements prepared by a company's private accountants. Consequently, to enhance the credibility of their organization's financial statements, company executives retain accounting firms to "audit" those statements to confirm that they have been prepared in accordance with generally accepted accounting principles. Exhibit 1 on page 6 presents an early audit report issued in the United States, Price Waterhouse's opinion on U.S. Steel's 1902 financial statements.

---

1. The Big Six firms include Arthur Andersen & Company, Coopers & Lybrand, Deloitte & Touche, Ernst & Young, KPMG Peat Marwick, and Price Waterhouse.

Exhibit 1 Price Waterhouse's Audit Opinion
on U.S. Steel's 1902 Financial Statements

We have examined the books of U.S. Steel Corporation
and its Subsidiary Companies for the year ending December 31, 1902, and certify that the Balance Sheet
at that date and the Relative Income Account are correctly prepared therefrom.

We have satisfied ourselves that during the year only
actual additions and extensions have been charged to
Property Account; that ample provision has been
made for Depreciation and Extinguishment, and that
the item of "Deferred Charges" represents expenditures reasonably and properly carried forward to operations of subsequent years.

We are satisfied that the valuations of the inventories
of stocks on hand as certified by the responsible officials have been carefully and accurately made at approximate cost; also that the cost of material and
labor on contracts in progress has been carefully

Most historians trace the beginning of the public
accounting profession in the United States to 1887
with the creation of the American Association of Public Accountants (AAPA), an organization that eventually became the American Institute of Certified Public
Accountants (AICPA). Although the AAPA had only
twenty-four charter members, within a few years after
its formation, it was significantly influencing the practice of public accountancy in the United States. The
lobbying efforts of the AAPA resulted in the passage

Exhibit 1 *(Continued)* Price Waterhouse's Audit Opinion on U.S. Steel's 1902 Financial Statements

ascertained, and that the profit on these contracts is fair and reasonable.

Full provision has been made for bad and doubtful accounts receivable and for all ascertainable liabilities.

We have verified the cash and securities by actual inspection or by certificates from the Depositories, and are of opinion that the Stocks and Bonds are fully worth the value at which they are stated in the Balance Sheet.

And we certify that in our opinion the Balance Sheet is properly drawn up so as to show the true financial position of the Corporation and its Subsidiary Companies, and that the Relative Income Account is a fair and correct statement of the net earnings for the fiscal year ending at that date.

of legislation regulating public accountancy in nearly all of the large industrialized states in the eastern and midwestern United States by the early 1900s. A century after the creation of the AAPA, the membership of the AICPA had swelled to more than 250,000 certified public accountants.

The rapid growth of the public accounting profession over the twentieth century was the most visible change that occurred in the profession within the United States during that time frame; however, other important changes have occurred within the profession in this country in recent decades. Some are still taking place. Many of these changes are in response to increasingly adverse conditions in the economic environment in which public accounting firms operate. The ability of accounting firms to cope with these adverse conditions will largely determine the societal role that public accountants will play in the twenty-first century.

CLOSING THE BOOKS ON THE 20TH CENTURY: MAJOR PROBLEMS FACING THE PUBLIC ACCOUNTING PROFESSION

The most pressing problem facing the public accounting profession as the twentieth century comes to a close is the dramatic increase in the number and magnitude of lawsuits filed against public accounting firms within the past two decades. Prior to the 1960s, civil suits against public accounting firms were relatively uncommon; by the early 1980s, however, lawsuits against public accounting firms were making headlines in the business press. Most of these lawsuits, particularly those in the multimillion dollar range, involved allegations of negligence during the performance of an independent audit by an accounting firm.

The legal problems of the public accounting profession worsened significantly with the near collapse of the savings and loan industry during the late 1980s and the related difficulties experienced by the banking industry. Accounting firms were sued for billions of dollars as a result of the financial crises in those two industries. These suits typically alleged that the audit reports issued on the financial statements of savings and loans, or banks that eventually failed should have alerted third parties that those institutions were in danger of failing. In other cases, these suits charged that auditors failed to discover that the financial health of a savings and loan or bank was being undermined by management fraud. In May 1992, Price Waterhouse was hit with a legal judgment of $338 million in one such case alone, a judgment that would have wiped out much of the firm's reported one-half billion dollars of partner capital. Fortunately for Price Waterhouse, the huge judgment was struck down in late 1992 by a federal judge who ordered that the case be retried. In November 1992, Ernst & Young, one of the largest, if not *the* largest, of the Big Six accounting firms, agreed to pay $400 million to the federal government to settle lawsuits stemming from the firm's audits of six failed savings and loans. However, approximately three-fourths of that amount was paid by Ernst & Young's insurers.

The cumulative litigation losses of the largest accounting firms in the United States over the past decade easily exceeded $1 billion. In fact, two of the fifteen largest United States accounting firms, Laventhol & Horwath and Spicer & Oppenheim, disbanded during the 1980s largely due to their litigation losses and the significant number of lawsuits still pending against them. In late 1990, Ernst & Young was forced to take out full-page ads in major metropolitan papers to counter rumors that it would be forced to dissolve because of its legal liability problems. In total, the public accounting profession, principally the

Big Six firms, was estimated to be facing approximately $15 billion in outstanding legal claims by early 1993.

Many prominent members of the public accounting profession blame the profession's mounting litigation problems on the United States judicial system, a system that allegedly encourages plaintiffs who suffer investment losses to file huge and often frivolous civil lawsuits against any "deep-pocketed" parties even remotely associated with their losses. Another prevalent view is that the profession's litigation problems stem from an "expectations gap" that has arisen between the consumers of accounting services and the firms that provide those services. That is, financial decision makers have higher expectations of public accountants than are justified given the legal and professional responsibilities assumed by public accountants. In the case of auditing services, for instance, a large proportion of financial statement users believe that auditors have a specific responsibility to discover and disclose instances in which business executives have fraudulently misrepresented their financial statements. However, such a responsibility has never been imposed explicitly on auditors. The public accounting profession has long resisted efforts by regulatory authorities to require auditors to discover management fraud, principally because fraudulent accounting schemes are very difficult to detect under most circumstances.

Given that an expectations gap exists between the public accounting profession and the consumers of accounting services, the issue becomes how to close that gap. The obvious alternatives are to either educate consumers regarding accountants' responsibilities or to redefine those responsibilities to align with the expectations of consumers. In the late 1980s, the public accounting profession attempted to close the expectations gap, at least with respect to the independent auditor's role. In 1988, the Auditing Standards Board adopted nine new technical standards, commonly referred to as the expectations gap standards, that imposed significant new responsibilities on independent auditors.

Another serious problem facing the public accounting profession is the increasing difficulty of convincing bright young men and women to consider accounting as a career choice. One indication of the declining quality of new recruits to the public accounting profession is the relatively poor performance of those individuals who have recently sat for the CPA exam. A recent study released by the National Association of State Boards of Accountancy demonstrated that "students are failing the CPA exam in record numbers." [2] That same study also reported that the percentage of CPA candidates with advanced degrees decreased from 13.5 percent in 1980 to 9.8 percent in 1990. Likewise, only 38.9 percent of CPA candidates in 1990 scored above 600 on the math section of the Scholastic Aptitude Test (SAT), while more than 60 percent of CPA candidates in 1975 posted a math SAT score exceeding 600.

Efforts of the profession to recruit potential accountants are often stymied by the perception that accounting is dull and uninteresting. Unfortunately, the press

---

2. J. Pickering, "Not Making the Grade: Record Percentage Flunks CPA Exam," *Accounting Today* (September 23, 1991): 1, 21.

reinforces this image with offhanded remarks about bureaucrats being "as imaginative as the average company accountant" and a meeting of state governors being "almost as exciting as a convention of certified public accountants." [3] Likewise, a published report in the *Wall Street Journal* that accountants represent the largest professional group in the "Dull Men's Club" of northern California does not contribute to a positive image of the public accounting profession.[4]

Apparently, many potential accountants share the public's unflattering image of accountants, an image that is largely undeserved. An early 1970s study, for instance, found that college students perceived accountants to be "low in status, conforming, lacking social skills, passive, weak, shallow, cold, submissive, and evasive." [5] A Gallup survey performed in 1991 indicated that college and college-bound students perceived accounting as the least important of six professional fields. That same study reported that high achievers in high school had less interest in pursuing a career in accounting than average and low achievers.[6]

In addition to recruitment problems, public accounting firms are losing many of their most highly qualified professionals to other fields, particularly to ac-

3. L. Berton, "Why You Never Saw Charles Bronson Cast As Hero Accountant," *Wall Street Journal* (April 26, 1984): 1, 21.

4. Ibid.

5. D.T. Decoster and J.G. Rhode, "The Accountant's Stereotype: Real or Imagined, Deserved or Unwarranted," *Accounting Review* vol. 46 (October 1971): 652.

6. *Journal of Accountancy*, "Gallup Study Finds Student Attitudes on CPA Careers Mixed," vol. 172, August 1991, 20–21.

counting positions in private industry. One prominent academic and former executive partner of a Big Six firm noted that this "brain drain" is likely related to the profession's present litigation crisis.[7] Unfortunately, the public accounting profession may be caught in a downward spiral. As the litigation problems of accounting firms worsen, they will likely see more of their highly qualified employees leaving public accounting for other fields which will further erode the quality of service provided by these firms. As the quality of their service diminishes, these firms can expect even more lawsuits to be filed against them. And so it goes.

LOOKING FORWARD TO THE 21ST CENTURY: CHALLENGES FACING THE PUBLIC ACCOUNTING PROFESSION

As the public accounting profession prepares to enter the next century, a number of challenges threaten its credibility, if not viability: resolving the litigation crisis, closing the expectations gap, and doing a more effective job of "selling" accounting as a career choice to young men and women. Two important and related challenges facing the public accounting profession are the need to monitor the rapidly changing needs of its clients and the need to "reach out" to

---

7. R. Telberg, "Audit Partner: Prince or Pariah?" *Accounting Today* (August 12, 1991): 3.

two important demographic groups that have apparently been slighted by the profession in the past.

The growing complexity of the business world is forcing financial decision makers such as investors, creditors, and regulatory authorities to rely increasingly on the expertise and advice of skilled professionals. These decision makers are continually demanding new types of financial services. As the demand for financial services has changed in recent years, so has the competitive nature of the market which provides those services. Public accounting firms are facing increasing competitive pressure from security analysts, personal financial planners, and related professional and quasi-professional groups. Several parties, including a number of prominent accountants, have suggested that public accounting firms are in danger of losing a significant portion of their share of the financial services market unless they do a better job of responding to the changing needs of the clients which they serve.[8]

In recent years, the public accounting profession has begun responding to the changing needs of financial decision makers by broadening the product line of services that it offers. For instance, until recently, accounting firms provided only one type of auditing service—an independent audit. However, now accounting firms provide three distinct types of auditing or auditing-related service, audits, "reviews," and "compilations." Reviews are essentially small-scale audits performed for companies that do not require an ex-

8. R.K. Mautz and H.A. Sharaf, *Philosophy of Auditing* (Sarasota, Florida: American Accounting Association, 1961).

tensive investigation of their financial statements but still require independent auditors to provide third parties with some degree of assurance regarding the integrity of those statements. Conversely, in a compilation engagement, an accounting firm simply prepares or compiles a set of financial statements for a client from the latter's accounting records.

In addition to reviews and compilations, public accounting firms have recently begun performing various types of "limited assurance" engagements and "attestation" engagements. Limited assurance engagements include: reviews of financial forecasts; reports on condensed financial statements; and so-called "agreed upon procedures" engagements which can involve reports by an accounting firm on practically any form of financial data. Possibly the greatest potential for revenue growth for public accounting firms lies in the provision of attestation services.

> An attest engagement is one in which a practitioner is engaged to issue or does issue a written communication that expresses a conclusion about the reliability of a written assertion that is the responsibility of another party.[9]

An example of an attest engagement was the retention by Wilson Sporting Goods of Coopers & Lybrand, a Big Six accounting firm, to support the company's claim that its Ultra golf ball is the "longest" golf ball off the tee. Accounting firms are also engaged to attest to the vote totals of contests and events of all types. For example, Price Waterhouse

---

9. *AICPA Professional Standards, Vol. 1* (Chicago: Commerce Clearing House, 1991), AT Section 100, para .01.

annually attests to the accuracy of the voting for the film industry's Academy Awards.

The most significant change that accounting firms have made to compete more effectively in the financial services industry of the future is a move toward providing a broad range of consulting services. For example, personal financial planning, litigation support services or forensic accounting, human resource management, design of cost control systems, and executive search services are just a few of the many consulting services that accounting firms now provide.

Tax return preparation is probably the type of service that consumers most commonly associate with public accountants. In the taxation field, as well as auditing and consulting, accounting firms are searching for ways to improve the quality of service they provide to their clients. Estate planning, structuring of sophisticated—and legal—tax shelters, assisting clients in complying with increasingly complex, if not convoluted, taxation laws, and minimizing taxes for multinational companies are among the more demanding challenges that will face tax practitioners in the next century.

The recent efforts of public accounting firms to respond to the changing needs of financial decision makers by providing a broader product line of services should enhance the competitive position of these firms in the financial services industry. In addition, accounting firms must ensure that the professional services they provide are of the highest quality possible. The most effective way to accomplish this objective is to hire the most highly qualified individuals available and then provide these individuals with the appropriate professional training. As noted earlier, however, the qualifications of college graduates entering public accounting have been declining in recent years. To counter this trend, the profession must do a better job of recruiting and retaining highly qualified members of two large demographic groups that have historically been underrepresented in public accounting, namely, women and minorities.

A 1976 Senate investigation of the personnel practices of the largest accounting firms in the nation demonstrated that both minorities and women were poorly represented at the top levels of those firms. The six accounting firms that supplied personnel data to the Senate had more than 3,500 partners. Of that total, only four were black males, while seven were white females. As a result of severe criticism of their hiring and promotion practices following the Senate investigation, the large public accounting firms undertook intensive efforts to recruit minorities and women.

By the late 1980s, women and minorities were being hired by the large accounting firms in considerable numbers for entry-level positions. However, both groups were still significantly underrepresented within the partnership ranks of these firms. For instance, in 1988 only 3.5 percent of the partnership positions of the eight largest accounting firms were held by women. Unless the profession does a better job of ensuring that their recruiting and promotion policies are color-blind and gender-blind, public accounting firms will find it increasingly difficult to convince highly qualified women and minorities to pursue careers in public accounting. Losing access to this large pool of talent would make it difficult for accounting firms to provide the highest quality of service and adversely affect their competitive position in the financial services industry.

IN SEARCH OF PACIOLI

In 1494, Pacioli recognized that merchants, the most important financial decision makers of his day, needed an efficient and cost effective means of processing financial information. Ever since, accountants have earned their livelihood by supplying reliable financial data to individuals and entities who need such information to make difficult decisions regarding the utilization of scarce resources. The future and success of the public accounting profession will ultimately be determined by whether or not the profession continues to recognize and satisfy the information needs of financial decision makers.

QUESTIONS

1. In your own words, define the factors that determine whether or not a field of endeavor qualifies as a profession.

2. Which of the following are "professional" work roles: politician, real estate agent, TV evangelist, major league baseball player, newspaper reporter, attorney. In your view, does public accounting qualify as a profession? Why or why not?

3. List the five work-related characteristics or attributes that will be most important to you when choos-

ing a career to pursue. To what degree are these factors present in public accounting?

4. The efforts of public accounting firms to broaden their product lines in recent years have been criticized by several parties, including certain public accountants. In particular, many critics suggest that by offering a broad array of financial services, including personal financial planning, human resource management, etc., accounting firms are moving away from those services which they are uniquely qualified to provide. Should accounting firms be allowed to provide any type of service they choose? Why or why not? If not, what limits should accounting firms impose on the types of services they provide?

5. Public accounting firms, particularly the large national firms, have been criticized for having disproportionally fewer women and minorities in top management positions. Should private partnerships, such as public accounting firms, be legally prohibited from discriminating against certain demographic groups in their hiring and promotion practices? Defend your answer.

6. Identify three specific tactics that accounting firms could utilize to attract and retain minorities and women.

7. Review the annual topical index of the *Wall Street Journal* or a major metropolitan newspaper for a recent year and identify an article or series of articles regarding a civil or criminal lawsuit filed against a public accounting firm. Write a short report which identifies the parties to this lawsuit and describes the basis of the lawsuit, that is, the allegations made against the CPA firm. If the relevant information is

available, summarize the resolution to the lawsuit. If that information is not available, briefly discuss the factors that will likely determine the outcome of the lawsuit.

Section Two

Accounting for Revenues and Expenses

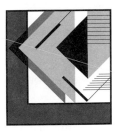

CASE 2.1
FLOWERS FOR
ALL OCCASIONS

In 1983, Florafax International, Inc., was the third largest company in the small "flowers-by-wire" industry. In fact, at the time, only six companies operated on a nationwide basis in the flowers-by-wire industry, the largest being FTD, Florists' Transworld Delivery Association. Founded in 1970 and headquartered in Tulsa, Oklahoma, Florafax operated a computerized network, Floracom, which connected retail florist shops across the nation. If a customer of a Philadelphia florist wanted to send flowers to someone in Dallas, the Philadelphia florist would write up the customer's order and then send it over the Floracom network to the Dallas-based florist located nearest the individual receiving the flowers. In a typical year, more than 80 percent of Florafax's revenues were generated by the 6 percent commissions it earned on orders placed over the Floracom network.

In the late 1970s and early 1980s, the top executives of Florafax were searching for ways to enhance the profitability of their company. Although Florafax's revenues had grown rapidly during the 1970s, the company's profits had not. In fact, in both 1979 and 1980, Florafax suffered losses exceeding $2.5 million on revenues of more than $34 million in 1979 and more than $44 million in 1980. To strengthen its competitive position, Florafax began acquiring small companies which provided services complementing its flowers-by-wire line of business. One of these new subsidiaries was a chain of seventy retail florist shops, For Love Flowers, located on military bases across the United States. Another Florafax acquisition, WhiskeyGram International, operated a "spirits-by-wire" service which allowed customers to wire alcoholic beverages to individuals across the nation. The largest of the companies acquired by Florafax in its expansion program was Garden Path Imports which sold silk flower arrangements and related products. By 1983, this subsidiary's sales accounted for more than 10 percent of Florafax's total revenues.

In addition to expanding the product line of their company, Florafax's executives adopted an aggressive marketing policy in the early 1980s to improve the company's operating results. One particularly successful marketing tactic was the holiday container program initiated in late 1980. Under this program, Florafax shipped silk flower arrangements, designed for specific holiday occasions by Garden Path Imports, to

Exhibit 1 Shipments Made by Florafax under its Holiday Container Program

Holiday	Number of Customers	Gross Sales
Christmas, 1980	2,258	$175,559
Secretary's Day, 1981	1,182	56,676
Easter, 1981	1,234	59,170
Mother's Day, 1981	8,562	598,515
Grandparents' Day, 1981	6,034	162,918
Thanksgiving, 1981	7,014	364,702
Christmas, 1981	6,973	661,088
Valentine's Day, 1982	5,510	264,456
Secretary's Day, 1982	6,575	631,200
Mother's Day, 1982	4,978	346,434

Source: Accounting and Auditing Enforcement Release No. 44, issued November 27, 1984, by the Securities and Exchange Commission.

selected retail florist shops nationwide. The retail florists receiving these shipments were shops which had good credit histories with Florafax and which had previously purchased silk flower arrangements from Garden Path Imports. As illustrated by Exhibit 1, Florafax made shipments of the holiday containers totalling several million dollars over a period of eighteen months.

Florafax also established a large-scale telemarketing program in 1981 to bolster its revenues and profits. In this program, Florafax sales personnel, using scripts written by top company executives, contacted

Exhibit 2 Selected Financial Data of Florafax, 1979–1983

	1983	1982	1981	1980	1979
Total revenues	$48,579	$50,981	$52,686	$44,439	$34,606
Income from continuing operations	2,100	1,338	1,134	(1,430)	(2,356)
Net income	2,724	2,410	2,080	(2,985)	(2,585)
Total assets	26,298	22,769	18,425	18,455	22,981

Source: 1983 Form 10–K registration statement filed with the Securities and Exchange Commission by Florafax International, Inc.

customers and encouraged them to place orders for various Florafax products. To increase the likelihood that customers would place orders, they were told that any items ordered could be returned for any reason, including inability to sell the products to their own retail customers.

The aggressive marketing policy adopted by Florafax's executives proved successful. As shown by Exhibit 2, the company went from a loss of nearly $3 million dollars in 1980 to a profit of more than $2 million the following year on significantly higher revenues. Even though Florafax's revenues declined somewhat in 1982 and 1983, the company posted healthy increases in net income for each of those years. Joseph Hale, who owned 28 percent of Florafax's outstanding common stock and served as the company's chief executive officer and chairman of the board, attributed the dramatic financial turnaround to the "aggressive marketing" plan that he and his associates had implemented.[1]

The impressive financial results posted by Florafax in the early 1980s drew the attention of investors and financial analysts nationwide. Following the company's resurgence, a financial analyst affiliated with a prominent investment firm reported in the *Wall Street Journal* that Florafax common stock was one of several small company stocks that his firm had targeted as excellent investment opportunities and was purchasing for the portfolios of its customers.[2] The financial turnaround orchestrated by Hale also drew the attention of the Securities and Exchange Commission (SEC) which regulates the financial reporting practices of publicly owned companies. In June 1983, the SEC contacted Florafax officials and informed them that an investigation of the company's financial affairs was under way. Nearly eighteen months later, the federal agency released a lengthy list of allegations which charged that Florafax had misrepresented its operating results during the early 1980s.

The focus of the SEC's investigation of Florafax was the aggressive marketing strategy adopted by the company in 1980. One key finding of the investigation was that the retail florists who participated in the holiday container program were not contacted by Florafax prior to being enrolled in that program. That is, these florists were simply shipped the holiday con-

1. *Wall Street Journal*, "Florafax Sees Profit Rise," (June 8, 1983): 24.

2. R.L. Rundle, "Stock Surge Is Seen by Two Money Managers Who Called the Turn in the Summer of 1982," *Wall Street Journal*, (June 28, 1984): 59.

tainer products without their prior approval. Failure to obtain customer authorization for these shipments resulted in an extremely high rate of sales returns as well as a deterioration in the relations between Florafax and its customers. A review of Florafax's accounting records revealed that the return rate for the holiday container products ranged from 28 percent to as high as 69 percent over the course of the program, return rates that were significantly higher than those previously experienced by the company.

In spite of the high return rates for the holiday container products, Florafax continued to make unauthorized shipments each subsequent holiday period to its customers. The SEC's principal concern regarding the program was not the fact that Florafax failed to obtain prior authorization for the shipments from its customers, but rather that the company immediately recorded the shipments as sales. According to the SEC, the immediate recording of these shipments as sales was inappropriate for a number of reasons.

> Florafax should not have recognized these revenues at the time of shipment since: neither a written or verbal sales agreement existed as to the automatic holiday shipments; the customer was under no obligation to pay Florafax for products which were shipped to him without authorization; the risk of loss had not passed to the customer; and, Florafax had no basis for reasonably estimating the rate of return of such unauthorized shipments.[3]

---

3. This and all subsequent quotes were taken from Accounting and Auditing Enforcement Release No. 44 issued November 27, 1984, by the Securities and Exchange Commission.

The SEC also took issue with the accounting procedures Florafax used for the sales generated by the
telemarketing program initiated by company officials
in 1981. Under that program, Florafax's customers
had an unconditional right to return any product
shipped to them. Apparently, this unconditional guar-
antee induced many of the company's customers to
place unreasonably large orders which resulted in a
huge increase in the return rate for Florafax's products. In fact, the return rate for Florafax's sales, ex-
cluding the holiday container sales, increased from 3
percent in 1980 to approximately 30 percent in 1981.

Finally, the SEC criticized Florafax officials for failing to disclose sufficient information regarding the
holiday container shipments and the 1981 telemarketing sales program in their company's periodic financial statements.

> In the management's discussion and analysis section of
> its Annual and Quarterly Reports for the fiscal years in-
> volved, Florafax failed to fairly and accurately disclose
> the different methods used . . . to market products,
> including the shipment and billing of products without
> customer authorization. Florafax also failed to disclose
> the magnitude of product returns which it experienced
> and the deterioration of its customer relations as a conse-
> quence of its product sales practices.

If the nature of Florafax's marketing practices and the
related accounting methods used in conjunction with
them had been adequately disclosed, readers of the
company's financial statements would likely have dis-
counted, to a large degree, the impressive financial
results reported by Florafax during the early 1980s.

The SEC charged that two officers of Florafax, Hale
and the company's controller, who was a certified

public accountant, had aided and abetted the misrepresentation of Florafax's financial condition and operating results. Each of these individuals was publicly reprimanded by the SEC, and Hale was required to resign as the company's chairman of the board and chief executive officer. In addition, Florafax agreed to recalculate Hale's compensation for 1981 and 1982. Since Hale's compensation in those years was based upon the pre-tax profits of Florafax, the SEC wanted to ensure that the company was repaid any amounts that he received as a result of the overstated earnings of the company. A final stipulation of the SEC's settlement with Florafax and its officers was that the company issue corrected financial statements for the years affected by the questionable marketing and accounting practices.

QUESTIONS

1. Assume that a Florafax customer ordered $200 of floral products on December 15, 1993, and that the customer had thirty days to pay for this order. The products sold to this customer had cost Florafax $120. On December 24, the customer sold one-half of these products for $150. Two weeks later, on January 7, 1994, the customer returned the remaining unsold products to Florafax because they were defective. Record the accounting entries that Florafax should have made to reflect these transactions in its accounting records assuming that the company uses a periodic inventory system.

2. In the facts provided for the prior question, assume that Florafax's fiscal year-end was December 31. Given this additional fact, how, if at all, were Florafax's reported profits for 1993 distorted by the series of transactions described above?

3. Assume that a company typically experiences a 5 percent return rate on its sales, but that it expects to experience a 20 percent return rate on a new product that it is marketing. Should the company employ a different accounting method for its normal returns versus the abnormally high returns it expects on the new product? Explain.

4. For the sales generated by Florafax's telemarketing program, the company's customers had an unconditional right to return the items purchased. If customers have an unconditional right to return purchased goods, when should a company recognize revenue on its sales transactions?

5. Florafax was reprimanded by the SEC for failing to provide sufficient information in its periodic financial statements regarding the holiday container shipments and the telemarketing sales program. One method that companies use to make their financial statements as informative as possible is to disclose important nonfinancial information in financial statement footnotes. Obtain several annual reports of public companies and review the footnotes appended to their financial statements. Then, draft a financial statement footnote for Florafax regarding its holiday container and telemarketing sales programs that would have remedied the SEC's concern that the company's financial statements failed to provide sufficient information regarding those programs.

CASE 2.2
DIMPLES DISCOS

Disco mania swept across the United States in the early 1970s fueled by the movie *Saturday Night Fever* and such disco tunes as "Jive Talkin'," "Kung Fu Fighting," and "Disco Duck." A number of companies saw an opportunity to capitalize on the disco fad by building discotheques. One of these companies was Emersons, Ltd., a publicly owned firm that operated a chain of steakhouses located primarily in New Jersey, Maryland, and the Washington, D.C., area. Emersons began building discotheques adjacent to many of its restaurants at the height of the disco frenzy. Management was hopeful that its Dimples Discos would attract additional customers to its restaurants and that sizable profits could be earned on liquor sales at the dance clubs. By the end of 1974,

Emersons had constructed twenty-six Dimples Discos, most of which were fully operational.

Founded in 1969 by John Radnay and headquartered in Rockville, Maryland, Emersons was one of the fastest growing companies in the "limited-menu" segment of the restaurant industry during the early 1970s. By 1974, Emersons was operating thirty-four restaurants with plans to open a dozen more. In that same year, the company reported profits of nearly $1 million on revenues of approximately $25 million. Only two years earlier, the company had reported a net income of $321,000 on revenues of slightly more than $6 million.

The bright prospects of Emersons were dimmed considerably in the mid–1970s when it was disclosed that federal authorities were investigating allegations that company officials had accepted illegal inducements from liquor companies. These inducements had reportedly been paid by the liquor companies to Radnay and other executives of Emersons to obtain exclusive rights to sell alcoholic beverages to the company's restaurants and discos. Matters worsened for Emersons when federal officials disclosed that their investigation had also uncovered possible irregularities in the company's financial records. Allegedly, Emersons' top executives had improperly accounted for several major expenditures to conceal the adverse effect on the company's profits of its aggressive expansion program in the early 1970s.[1]

---

1. Most of the background material for this case was taken from Accounting and Auditing Enforcement Release No. 288, issued February 26, 1981, by the Securities and Exchange Commission.

The principal allegation regarding Emersons' financial recordkeeping was that from 1972 through 1975, the company had deferred or capitalized several large expenditures on its year-end balance sheets that should have been recognized as expenses on its annual income statements. Generally accepted accounting principles (GAAP), specifically the "matching principle," require that expenditures be recognized as expenses on an entity's income statement in the accounting period in which they provide an economic benefit to the entity. Typically, this means that an expenditure should be treated as an expense in the period in which it results in revenue being generated for the entity in question. When an expenditure provides a discernible economic benefit to several future periods, the amount involved should be capitalized and then written off as an expense on a pro rata basis to those future periods.

The matching principle is often difficult to apply, particularly when there is no clear cause and effect relationship between an expenditure and the subsequent revenue that it generates. For instance, in the case of a large factory, it would be unreasonable to expect company executives to determine exactly how much of the cost of the factory to expense each year of operation since the productive life of the factory would be difficult, if not impossible, to estimate with any degree of precision. Pharmaceutical companies which engage in long-term, multimillion dollar research programs to develop new products have a similar but even more difficult problem. Matching the cost of those programs with the subsequent revenues they generate is essentially impossible given the unpredictability inherent in the process of developing

Exhibit 1 Expenditures that Were Improperly Capitalized by Emersons

Expenditure	Justification for Capitalizing
Pre-opening costs: training costs incurred for new employees	These costs were necessary to create a skilled work crew which would enhance the productivity and profitability of a new operating unit for several years.
Advertising expenditures incurred in the first few months of a new unit's operations	The advertising expenses incurred in the first few months of a new unit's operations benefited future accounting periods by creating a clientele for that unit.
Software development costs: salaries and related payroll costs of all employees working on a large software development project	The software developed by Emersons' personnel would benefit the company indefinitely by providing a more effective system of accounting and administrative controls.

and marketing new pharmaceuticals. When there is no clear cause and effect relationship between an expenditure and the subsequent revenues of an entity, the conservatism principle inherent in GAAP dictates that the expenditure be recognized as an expense in the period that it is incurred.

Exhibit 1 lists five types of expenditures that Emersons improperly capitalized in the early 1970s and the rationale for the accounting treatment accorded each

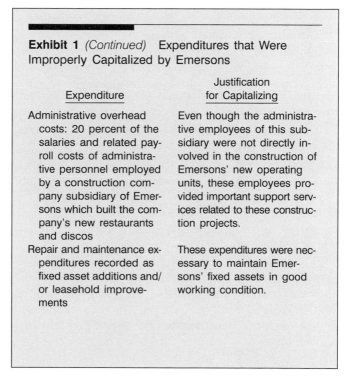

Exhibit 1 *(Continued)* Expenditures that Were Improperly Capitalized by Emersons

Expenditure	Justification for Capitalizing
Administrative overhead costs: 20 percent of the salaries and related payroll costs of administrative personnel employed by a construction company subsidiary of Emersons which built the company's new restaurants and discos	Even though the administrative employees of this subsidiary were not directly involved in the construction of Emersons' new operating units, these employees provided important support services related to these construction projects.
Repair and maintenance expenditures recorded as fixed asset additions and/or leasehold improvements	These expenditures were necessary to maintain Emersons' fixed assets in good working condition.

of those items. Of course, by capitalizing these expenditures, that is, debiting them to asset accounts rather than recording them directly in expense accounts, Emersons' management inflated the reported profits of the company and increased the attractiveness of the company's stock to investors.

Emersons' accounting for the expenditures shown in Exhibit 1 was a focal point of the federal investigation of the company. In May 1976, the Securities and

Exchange Commission (SEC) appointed Francis T. Vincent to serve as Special Counsel in the investigation of the alleged criminal activity of Emersons' executives and the alleged irregularities in the company's publicly released financial statements. Vincent, who years later would become the commissioner of major league baseball, retained the accounting firm of Touche Ross & Company to perform an extensive audit of Emersons' accounting records for the early 1970s. Largely as a result of the evidence collected by Touche Ross, the SEC ruled that the accounting treatment accorded each of the expenditures shown in Exhibit 1 was improper.

Regarding the "pre-opening" training costs deferred by Emersons, the SEC disclosed that the majority of these expenditures were actually incurred after the opening of new restaurants and discos, and, consequently, did not qualify as pre-opening costs. Although an argument could be made that "post-opening" employee training costs provide a company with future economic benefits, the SEC concluded that such a contention was tenuous, at best, and that the costs in question should have been immediately expensed in the period incurred. To support its position on this issue, the SEC noted that most companies in the restaurant industry immediately expense all payroll-related costs incurred by operating units subsequent to their opening, including training costs.[2]

---

2. In fact, capitalizing actual "pre-opening costs" is a questionable practice since it is difficult to establish a strong cause and effect relationship between such expenditures and subsequent revenues of an entity.

The SEC also ruled that Emersons was not justified in deferring or capitalizing advertising expenditures made on behalf of a new operating unit since it was difficult to establish that such expenditures yielded a clearly discernible economic benefit to future accounting periods. Again, to support its stance on this issue, the SEC reviewed the accounting practices of Emersons' competitors. The SEC noted that only one other company in the industry was found to have capitalized advertising expenditures incurred on behalf of a new operating unit.

The SEC did not contest the right of Emersons to capitalize costs associated with the development of software to be used internally in the company's new management information system. However, the results of the SEC's investigation disclosed that a large portion of the costs capitalized in connection with that project were actually operational costs incurred after the software was in use by the company. Operational costs of a new computer system are clearly not capitalizable, the SEC maintained, since they benefit only the accounting period in which they are incurred.

The SEC also did not contest the right of Emersons to capitalize a portion of the administrative overhead expenses incurred by the subsidiary that constructed the company's new restaurants and discos. However, the federal agency ruled that Emersons had capitalized an excessive portion of those expenditures. Rather than capitalizing 20 percent of the administrative expenses in question, the SEC concluded that Emersons should have capitalized only 10 percent.

During the course of Touche Ross's audit of Emersons' financial records, the accounting firm discov-

ered that more than $200,000 of repair and mainte-
nance expenditures had been capitalized by the company. According to GAAP, repair and maintenance
expenditures should not be capitalized but rather
treated as expenses in the period incurred. One exception to this general rule is when repair and maintenance expenditures extend the useful life of an asset.
In such a case, it is common to debit the cost of the
expenditures to the accumulated depreciation account
of the given asset rather than debiting the amount
directly to the asset account. The SEC ruled that the
repair and maintenance expenditures incurred by
Emersons did not extend the useful life of the assets
in question and, consequently, should have been
treated as expenses for accounting purposes.

The results of the SEC's investigation of Emersons
resulted in the company being required to issue corrected financial statements for 1974 and 1975. In each
of those years, the restated net income figure of the
company was approximately 50 percent below the
amount initially reported. The SEC also forced John
Radnay to resign as president and chairman of the
board of Emersons and ousted the company's treasurer as well. In March 1978, Radnay settled the criminal charges outstanding against him by pleading
guilty to one count of filing a false income tax return
and one count of filing false financial statements with
the SEC. A guilty plea was also obtained by federal
authorities in the Emersons case from the president of
the New Jersey State Senate who admitted paying a
bribe to the company to obtain the exclusive right to
sell liquor to the Emersons restaurants and discos in
New Jersey.

Unfortunately for Emersons, disco mania proved to be a relatively short-lived phenomenon. By the end of 1975, Emersons had closed all but six of its Dimples Discos. Two years later, the company filed for protection from its creditors under the federal bankruptcy statutes.

QUESTIONS

1. Emersons violated the "conservatism principle" in accounting for several types of expenditures. Does this principle apply to accounting decisions involving revenues? If so, briefly discuss how the conservatism principle might affect a company's accounting decisions for the following revenue accounts: credit sales of merchandise, interest income, revenue on long-term construction contracts.

2. Emersons also violated the "matching principle" in accounting for certain expenditures. For the following three situations, apply the matching principle properly to determine how to account for the given expenses.

a. Assume that a company sells a product with a five-year parts and labor warranty. How should the company account for the expenses that it expects to incur as a result of the product warranty?

b. Assume that a company sells large, precooked hams. Near the end of a given year, the company has a marketing promotion ending December 31st for this product which allows customers to receive a $2 refund for each proof of purchase that they send the company. Assume that the company pays 10,000 of the refunds prior to December 31st and estimates that another 40,000 will be paid the following year. How should these refunds be recorded for accounting purposes?

c. A large consulting company sends its newly hired employees through an intensive, twelve-week training program. The cost of this program is approximately $10,000 per employee. Prior to entering the program, the new employees sign a contract promising to repay the company $8,000 if they complete the program and then leave the company during the first year of their employment, $5,000 if they leave the company during the second year of their employment, and $2,500 if they leave the company during the third year of their employment. If an employee remains with the company for three or more years following the completion of the training program, he or she has no financial obligation to the company. Assume that the company sends ten employees through its training program at the beginning of 1995. How should the company account for the $100,000 in costs incurred to train these new employees?

3. Assume for purposes of this question that Emersons reported the following net income amounts for the period 1972–1975: 1972—$300,000; 1973—$600,000; 1974—$1,000,000; 1975—$1,200,000. Also assume that the following table lists the total amount of expenditures improperly capitalized by the company for the years indicated and that each of these expenditures was amortized over a period of four years.

	1972	1973	1974	1975
Pre-opening costs	$100,000	$200,000	$300,000	$300,000
Advertising expenditures	60,000	—	—	80,000
Software development costs	—	—	200,000	200,000
Administrative overhead costs	80,000	—	—	100,000
Repair and maintenance expenditures	—	200,000	—	—

If Emersons' effective tax rate during the early 1970s was 40 percent, calculate the correct net income figure for each of the above years.

Case 2.3

The Bottom Line:
Accounting Earnings
vs. Economic Income

Hand a set of financial statements to a stockholder, a banker, a security analyst, or any other financial decision maker and more often than not that individual will turn immediately to the income statement and locate the earnings per share figure. Should I invest in this company? Will this company be able to repay a loan for which it has applied? Should the officers of the company be retained? These are among the critical questions that decision makers pose when they study a set of financial statements. Although the earnings per share figure reported in the income statement will not, by itself, determine the answers to those questions, that figure is practically always an important factor in the financial statement user's ultimate decision.

Unfortunately, many, if not most, financial statement users have the false impression that published earnings figures are precise measures of profitability, an impression formed by the precision with which those figures are reported to the public. If IBM and Exxon, companies with billions of dollars of assets, report that their earnings for a given period of time are $5.47 and $3.61 per share, respectively, it is not unreasonable for Joe Q. Public to conclude that earnings figures can be precisely determined to the nearest penny. In fact, as any accountant knows, accounting earnings are no more than "guesstimates" of actual profits.

In recent years, accountants have faced increasing criticism for the manner in which they measure an entity's profitability over a given period of time. At the core of this controversy is a lack of agreement on how to define income. Probably the most widely accepted definition of income by economists is the change in an entity's "well-offness" from the beginning to the end of a period of time.[1] This concept of economic income assumes that the measurement of profitability is essentially a valuation process. That is, once you determine the net value of an entity at the beginning and end of an accounting period, the difference between those two figures is the entity's in-

---

1. S. Cottle, R.F. Murray, and F.S. Block, *Graham and Dodd's Security Analysis* (New York: McGraw–Hill, 1988): 138.

come or earnings for that period of time. Accountants, however, have historically used a much different approach to measuring income. Instead of defining net income as the change in value of an entity between two points in time, accountants measure profitability by analyzing the transactions that occurred during a given accounting period. Under generally accepted accounting principles (GAAP) and the accrual basis of accounting, net income is the difference between an entity's revenues and expenses with certain adjustments for various "non-transaction" items, such as estimates of bad debt expense for accounts receivable and depreciation on buildings and other fixed assets.

Among the parties most critical of the accounting profession's approach to earnings measurement are security analysts. Because they serve as financial consultants to literally tens of millions of individuals who are less than knowledgeable of accounting rules and concepts, security analysts are probably the most important users of the periodic financial statements prepared by accountants. For decades, security analysts, both individually and as a group, have called for accountants to provide earnings figures that more closely approximate the economic incomes of reporting entities. Research studies by academics, numerous litigation cases focusing on the reported earnings of public and private companies, and enforcement actions taken against companies by regulatory authorities tend to corroborate security analysts' allegations that the "true" income of a reporting entity for a period of time is often significantly different from the earnings figure it releases to the general public.

MEASUREMENT PROBLEMS WITH ACCOUNTING EARNINGS

One of the primary needs of economic decision makers is financial data prepared on a consistent basis across companies, particularly companies within the same industry. Unfortunately, the large number of acceptable accounting principles for any given type of transaction or financial statement item often results in reported earnings figures that are not comparable, even across companies that are very similar. For instance, a given company may use the first-in, first-out (FIFO) method to account for its inventory and calculate depreciation on its fixed assets using the straight-line depreciation method, while a competing company in the same industry uses the last-in, first-out (LIFO) method for inventory and calculates depreciation using an accelerated method. Even if the true economic incomes of these firms are identical, their reported earnings are unlikely to be comparable because of the different set of accounting methods they employ.

The increasing trend toward the internationalization of business enterprises will cause financial statement users even more difficulty in comparing the earnings figures of companies. To illustrate the significant differences in accounting rules across developed countries, three accounting professors calculated the net income of a company with a gross profit of $1.5 million, assuming the company was domiciled in four different countries, the United States, the United Kingdom, Australia, and West Germany. The net income figures ranged from $10,402 in West Germany to approximately $250,000 in both the United Kingdom and Australia. In the United States, the hypothetical company would have reported a net income of $34,600.[2]

Another limitation of accounting-derived measures of periodic income is that GAAP does not capture or quantify all of the information that affects the change in the economic value of an entity from one period to the next. One observer of the accounting profession commented on this critical limitation of accounting's approach to earnings measurement.

> It would be wonderful if accounting were one of the exact sciences that observes all variables, measures them with whatever degree of accuracy is needed, and presents a final number that all would agree was 'economic reality' . . . [However,] accounting simply measures what it *can* observe and measure, which is mostly exchange transactions in which the company was a party.[3]

Because of the conservatism principle, for instance, accountants ignore so-called "gain contingencies," events or circumstances that may result in considerable profit accruing to an entity in the future. Likewise, accountants, in most cases, ignore changes in the market value of an entity's assets from one period to the next. Finally, accounting does not have a mechanism for capturing or quantifying the change in value of many intangible, off-balance sheet assets, such as the human resources of an organization.

---

2. L. Berton, "No Comparisons: The Bottom Line is that Accounting and Disclosure Rules Overseas are a Minefield for the Uninitiated," *Wall Street Journal* (September 22, 1989): R30.

3. *Graham and Dodd's Security Analysis*, 137.

Arguably, the principal reason that accounting earnings are a poor surrogate for economic income is the incentive and ability of business executives to manipulate or "manage" reported profits for their own benefit. Unfortunately, the inherent flexibility of GAAP often facilitates such efforts to distort a company's financial statements and thus misrepresent its economic reality. Executives are particularly tempted to engage in earnings management when their company has an incentive compensation plan linked to reported profits. For example, in the late 1970s, United States Surgical Corporation, a leading supplier of surgical instruments, adopted an incentive compensation plan that paid its officers a significant bonus if the company's profits were 15 to 30 percent above the prior year's reported profits. In 1981, the company's earnings increased 27 percent which resulted in large bonuses accruing to its officers. However, a subsequent investigation by the Securities and Exchange Commission (SEC) disclosed that United States Surgical's officers had intentionally overstated the company's earnings to allow them to collect payments under the bonus plan.

The most common form of earnings management is probably "income smoothing" which has been defined as the "dampening of fluctuations about some level of earnings that is considered normal for a firm." [4] Research studies suggest that executives attempt to "smooth" earnings from period to period

---

4. C. Beidleman, "Income Smoothing: The Role of Management," *Accounting Review*, vol. 48 (October 1973): 653–67.

because they have a strong preference for a stable earnings trend rather than one which is characterized by significant volatility.[5] For instance, assume that Company A and Company B are very similar in all respects and that each had cumulative earnings of $300,000 over a five-year period as shown by the table below. In spite of the fact that the two firms had the same earnings over the five-year period, from the standpoint of business executives the earnings trend of Company A would be preferred to that of Company B.[6] The volatile nature of Company B's earnings would almost certainly result in that firm being charged a higher interest rate than Company A to borrow funds from a bank. Bankers would be much more comfortable with extending a loan to Company A since its earnings appear more predictable than those of Company B and thus easier to extrapolate into the future. In addition, to protect their own economic self-interests, executives would prefer Company A's earnings trend since their job security would be threatened by the net loss posted by Company B in 1992 and possibly by the modest net income earned by that firm in 1994.

---

5. B. Trueman, and S. Titman, "An Explanation for Accounting Income Smoothing," *Journal of Accounting Research*, vol. 26 (Supplement 1988): 127–43.

6. This comparison ignores tax implications and present value considerations.

	1991	1992	1993	1994	1995
Company A, Net Income	$48,000	$59,000	$58,000	$64,000	$71,000
Company B, Net Income	$92,000	($3,000)	$98,000	$34,000	$79,000

Exhibit 1 lists several methods that corporate management may use either to achieve a pre-determined earnings goal for a given accounting period or to smooth earnings from one period to the next. The various methods of earnings management listed in Exhibit 1 can be grouped into three general catego-

Exhibit 1 Examples of Earnings Management Techniques

Income Statement Account Affected	Technique
Cost of goods sold	Selling inventory items that have the lowest per unit cost to maximize gross profit
Research and development expenditures	Capitalizing rather than expensing R & D expenditures
Maintenance expenses	Postponing scheduled maintenance expenses on production equipment until the following accounting period
Capital gains on marketable securities	Selling securities that have increased significantly in value while retaining securities whose value has fallen

ries. The first type includes what are known as "real" earnings management techniques. When using this form of earnings management, executives purposefully modify an operating decision to influence the reported earnings of their firm. An example of such a technique would be the postponement of year-end maintenance expenditures scheduled on production equipment. Of course, the postponement of such expenses is likely to have a negative economic effect on the firm over the long run since the production equipment will be more likely to break down, resulting in

Exhibit 1 *(Continued)* Examples of Earnings Management Techniques

Income Statement Account Affected	Technique
Operating expenses	Treating operating expenses as nonoperating or nonrecurring items for income statement purposes
Sales	Recording sales orders received in the last few days of a fiscal year as consummated sales transactions even though the goods will not be shipped until the following fiscal year
Depreciation expense	Arbitrarily extending the estimated useful lives of assets to reduce their periodic depreciation expense

disrupted production schedules and possibly lost sales. However, when executives engage in earnings management they are typically willing to accept lower profits over the long run in exchange for being able to manipulate third parties' perceptions of their firm's current operating results.

The second general type of earnings management involves company executives taking advantage of the inherent flexibility of GAAP. For example, if it appears that a company will fall short of its target profit goal for a given period, management may begin intentionally selling inventory items that are recorded on the company's books at relatively low per unit costs. This form of earnings management is particuarly feasible if a company employs the LIFO method of inventory valuation. When using LIFO, a company will quite often have inventory items carried on its books at per unit prices that are several years old. For instance, the per unit cost to replace an inventory item may be $10 even though the LIFO cost recorded on the books for that item is only $3. By deferring inventory purchases, management can ensure that inventory items that have an outdated, and relatively low, per unit cost attached to them are sold, resulting in a much larger than normal gross profit on sales.

A final form of earnings management involves fraudulent conduct on the part of a company's executives or their subordinates. Backdating sales made during the first week of a new fiscal year so that the sales appear to have been made in the final week of the prior fiscal year is a fraudulent scheme that financially distressed companies sometimes use to overstate their revenues and earnings.

ASSESSING THE QUALITY OF REPORTED EARNINGS

Security analysts have long recognized that accounting earnings figures are often not good substitutes for economic income. In response to this realization, many security analysts maintain that both the quantity and quality of the accounting earnings reported by companies should be assessed.[7] Although the concept of "earnings quality" is not rigidly defined, the term is most frequently used to express the degree of correlation between a firm's accounting earnings and its true economic income. Security analysts are very interested in a firm's economic income since it is assumed to be a much better predictor than accounting earnings of the future cash flows that the firm will generate, future cash flows being the ultimate determinant of the economic value of an entity. Exhibit 2 lists some of the standard analytical techniques used by security analysts to evaluate the quality of a firm's reported earnings.

Most of the techniques shown in Exhibit 2 on page 56 are intended to determine whether the executives of a given company have utilized one or more of the three forms of earnings management discussed earlier to manipulate their firm's reported earnings. For instance, changes in accounting principles that increase earnings and reductions in discretionary expenditures

---

7. *Forbes*, "Quality vs. Quantity" (February 1, 1977): 71; P. Dreyfus, "Go With the (cash) Flow," *Institutional Investor*, (August 1988): 55–57.

Exhibit 2 Measures to Use in Assessing the Quality of Reported Earnings

1. Compare accounting principles employed by a given company to those used by competitors. Does the set of accounting principles used by the company tend to inflate reported earnings?

2. Analyze any recent changes in accounting principles or accounting estimates to determine whether they inflated reported earnings.

3. Determine whether discretionary expenditures, such as advertising and maintenance expenses, have decreased significantly during the period in question.

4. Attempt to determine whether there are any significant expenses not reflected in the company's income statement, such as warranty expenses on products sold by the company.

5. Analyze the replacement cost of inventories and other assets to determine whether the company's operations are generating sufficient cash flow to replenish inventory and to replace other assets at the end of their productive lives.

may signal that management is attempting to artificially inflate earnings. If the reported earnings of a company have been manipulated, their correlation with the firm's economic income will be diminished.

Several of the measures listed in Exhibit 2 are used by security analysts to determine whether an entity's financial statements have failed to capture the eco-

Exhibit 2 *(Continued)* Measures to Use in Assessing the Quality of Reported Earnings

6. Read the footnotes to the financial statements to determine whether any major loss contingencies exist which could negatively affect future earnings.

7. Analyze nonoperating expenses or losses included in the income statement and determine whether they are actually nonoperating items.

8. Analyze the relationship between sales and receivables. Are receivables increasing more rapidly than sales?

9. Determine whether significant related party transactions could have resulted in an overstatement of revenues and earnings.

10. Read the "management's discussion and analysis" section of the annual report to obtain insight on management's view of the company's operations, and review the independent auditor's report to identify any major accounting issues or problems uncovered by the company's auditors.

nomic reality of its operating results even in the absence of explicit earnings management by company executives. For instance, analysis of the replacement costs of a company's productive assets may disclose that although the company is profitable, its future cash flows may not be sufficient to provide for the replacement of those assets in the future. Likewise, a company's sales may be increasing significantly, resulting in an impressive increase in reported earnings; however, if the increase in sales was accomplished by accepting customers who are high credit risks, the company may be unable to collect its accounts receivable when they come due. Comparison of the growth rates of sales and accounts receivable would provide clues as to whether revenue recognized on sales transactions will eventually result in cash inflows for the company.

Once a financial statement user has analyzed the quality of a company's reported earnings by using the techniques shown in Exhibit 2, the next step is to make the appropriate adjustments in the reported earnings figure to arrive at an approximate estimate of the company's true economic income. This latter figure can then be used, along with any other pertinent information, to reach a more informed decision regarding such questions as whether to loan the company funds or whether to invest in the company's stock.

Improving the Quality of Accounting Earnings

Unless the accounting profession takes steps to improve the quality of accounting earnings figures, the credibility of accounting data and the entire financial reporting process will continue to erode. One prominent academic warns that corporate executives, because of the flexibility of GAAP, may eventually be able to manage accounting numbers to the "point of uninformativeness." [8] One of the most obvious measures the profession can take to enhance the quality of accounting earnings figures is to narrow the range of acceptable accounting alternatives for inventory, receivables, and other important financial statement items. Of course, such standardization would be meaningless unless rule-making bodies ensure that only accounting principles that capture economic reality are permitted to be used. Another measure to increase the quality of accounting earnings would be to encourage companies not to adopt incentive compensation plans for their top executives. Prohibiting or restricting the use of such plans would eliminate one of the principal motives for corporate executives to manipulate their companies' accounting data.

The SEC is one regulatory body that is reacting to the criticism of accounting-derived earnings figures. Recently, the SEC suggested that the accounting profession consider replacing historical cost-based accounting with current value accounting. The use of current values for balance sheet reporting purposes would greatly facilitate efforts to move toward a definition of accounting earnings that more closely approximates economic income. The SEC has also intensified its efforts to enforce current regulations that prohibit companies from intentionally producing and distributing misleading financial data, including distorted earnings figures. The sanctions imposed on top officials of United States Surgical Corporation for manip-

---

8. K. Schipper, "Commentary on Earnings Management," *Accounting Horizons*, vol. 3 (December 1989): 91.

ulating their company's reported earnings is an example of numerous enforcement actions taken by the SEC in recent years against corporate executives who have released misleading earnings figures to the general public.

QUESTIONS

1. One of the earnings management techniques listed in Exhibit 1 is the treatment of operating expenses as nonoperating expenses for income statement purposes. Since both operating and nonoperating expenses reduce a company's reported profits, what earnings management objective would this technique accomplish?

2. Assume that ABC Company sold 1,000 units of product X at a per unit price of $10 and that these units had been purchased at a cost of $6 per unit. The replacement cost of each of these units is now $8. Ignoring all other variables, how much income did ABC Company earn as a result of this transaction? Explain.

3. Assume that on January 1, 1995, JKL Company signs a contract to supply military uniforms to the federal government. JKL will deliver 40,000 uniforms to the U.S. Army each year from 1996 through 1999. During 1995, the company will design the uniforms and construct the equipment that will be used to manufacture them. If JKL expects to realize a net profit of $1.6 million on the contract, how do you believe that profit should be allocated to the years 1995 through 1999? Explain your reasoning.

4. Among the largest groups of financial statement users are stockholders and bondholders. Briefly discuss the different issues or concerns that these two groups of financial statement users would likely focus upon when evaluating financial data. In your answer, identify the facet of given entities' financial performance which would be of most interest to stockholders and the facet which would be of most concern to bondholders.

5. Researchers have documented that business executives often intentionally overstate expenses when a company is experiencing a very poor year financially, resulting in an even larger loss for the company. What motivates this type of behavior? Is such behavior inconsistent with the use of income smoothing tactics by business executives? Explain.

6. In recent years, the accounting profession has attempted to increase the usefulness of financial statement data by requiring that companies include a statement of cash flows in their annual financial statement package. Compare and contrast the usefulness of accounting earnings and cash flow information in assessing the future prospects of a company.

7. Research the differences that exist between the accounting principles used in a specific foreign country and the United States. Identify at least five such differences. Write a report summarizing the results of your research. In your report, discuss why these differences exist and comment on the impact they have on the comparability of financial statements prepared in the two countries.

SECTION THREE

CRITICAL ACCOUNTING DECISIONS FOR ASSETS

Case 3.1
Accounting,
Lies, and Videotape

Video rental stores began popping up in communities of all sizes across the United States in the late 1970s following the introduction of the video cassette recorder (VCR) by Sony Corporation in 1977. Suddenly, the fans of the "big screen" who could afford the sizable price tag of the early VCRs were able to enjoy their favorite movies as often as they desired in the comfort of their own homes. By the late 1980s, the average price of a VCR had fallen to a few hundred dollars, enabling families with even modest incomes to participate in the "home video revolution." In fact, by 1990, more than 60 million households in the

United States had at least one VCR, and monthly video cassette rentals were approaching 150 million.

Like many new industries, the video rental industry quickly reached a point of maturation at which the rate of growth of its total revenues and profits began to decrease. Although the number of VCR households and the number of monthly video cassette rentals continued to increase into the early 1990s, the profitability of many, if not most, companies in the industry had been declining for several years. Most of this decline was due to the increasingly competitive nature of the industry. The ease of entry into the video rental industry prompted large numbers of opportunistic but undercapitalized entrepreneurs to open small video rental stores, many of which survived for no more than a few months. At the same time the number of video rental outlets was increasing, the average number of video rentals per household was falling. In 1986, each VCR household rented 3.3 video cassettes per month; by late 1991, that figure had dropped to less than 2.1. As one analyst noted, the major problem facing the industry in the early 1990s was the fact that the VCR was no longer a novelty for most American households. "In the 1980s, the VCR was a new toy; in 1990, it is a familiar extension of the television set." [1]

One of the companies that pioneered the video rental industry was a California-based firm, The Video Station. Founded in 1977 by two brothers, George and Edward Atkinson, the company had

---

1. P.M. Nichols, "Movie Rentals Fade, Forcing an Industry To Change its Focus," *New York Times* (May 6, 1991): 1, 34.

more than 550 retail rental outlets by the mid–1980s. The Video Station was apparently the first video rental company to offer a full line of video-related services and products, including video cassette rentals, VCR rentals, video camera rentals, blank video tapes, video games, etc. George Atkinson, the company's president, noted in his firm's first annual report that his objective was to create a chain of one-stop-shopping home video speciality stores to take advantage of the voracious appetite of VCR owners for video-related services and products.

In the first few years of The Video Station's existence, its revenues and assets grew explosively. In just three years, from 1979 to 1982, the company's annual revenues went from approximately $1.4 to nearly $14 million, while its total assets increased from $208,000 to nearly $7 million. As the video rental industry became increasingly crowded, however, The Video Station began to experience downward pressure on its earnings. In 1982, to raise much needed working capital, the Atkinson brothers decided to sell additional common stock in their publicly owned company. To comply with federal securities laws, The Video Station's executives prepared a registration statement, commonly referred to as a prospectus, for the nearly one million shares of stock they intended to sell. The registration statement filed with the Securities and Exchange Commission (SEC) contained financial statements for The Video Station that had been audited by the company's accounting firm.

Unknown to the SEC at the time, the 1981 and 1982 financial statements of The Video Station that were included in the company's prospectus materially misrepresented the firm's financial condition and results of operations. The Atkinson brothers had apparently been concerned that their ability to sell The Video Station common stock would be impaired if the true financial condition and operating results of the company were disclosed to the public. Consequently, the two executives, with the assistance of certain of the company's accountants, distorted the reported financial data of The Video Station by applying a number of improper accounting methods.

One of the largest assets of a video rental concern is its investment in video cassettes. By the early 1980s, The Video Station, like many of its major competitors, had begun selling video cassettes to the public in addition to renting them. Generally accepted accounting principles (GAAP) mandate that different accounting methods be used for assets that are held for sale to customers versus those that are rented to customers. Video cassettes held for sale are required to be included in a current asset account, typically labeled inventory, while video cassettes held for rental purposes are considered a noncurrent asset and included under the heading of property, plant and equipment on an entity's balance sheet.

The executives of The Video Station realized that any video cassettes reported as noncurrent assets on the company's balance sheet would have to be depreciated. Conversely, GAAP does not require that depreciation be recorded on assets held for sale in the ordinary course of an entity's operations. By reporting video cassettes held for rental purposes as inventory, rather than as property, plant and equipment, the company's executives avoided recording depreciation on these assets, and, as a result, distorted both The Video Station's balance sheet and its income statement. The company's balance sheet was misrepresented since the video cassettes that were being rented were reported at original historical cost rather than historical cost less accumulated depreciation. The company's income statement was misstated since it failed to include the required depreciation charges on the video cassettes held for rental purposes.

For the video cassettes that The Video Station held for sale to customers, the company was required to determine whether the net realizable value of those cassettes was less than their historical cost. If the historical cost of these video cassettes exceeded their net realizable value, GAAP required that they be written down to the latter amount. In fact, inventory obsolescence was a major problem for The Video Station and its competitors. The difficulty of predicting the public's taste in motion pictures often results in video rental stores being "stuck" with a large number of video cassettes that customers neither want to rent or purchase. To provide for more impressive financial statements for their company, the executives of The Video Station ignored the inventory obsolescence issue and reported the video cassettes held for sale at historical cost rather than the lower of historical cost or net realizable value.

The net effect of the improper accounting methods for the investments in video cassettes and the related financial statement items of The Video Station were significant overstatements of the company's reported net income for 1981 and 1982 as shown by the following table. These irregularities in The Video Station's financial statements were discovered as a result of an investigation into the company's financial affairs by the SEC.

	1981	1982
Net Income initially reported by The Video Station	$79,304	$204,474
Restated Net Income following SEC investigation	$(214,000)	$(890,000)

The SEC's investigation disclosed that the chief financial officer (CFO) of The Video Station had been involved in the scheme to manipulate the company's financial statements. The CFO, who was a CPA and had previously been employed by the accounting firm that audited The Video Station, was hired by the Atkinson brothers in June 1982. At the time he accepted a position with the company, the CFO was unaware of the fraudulent accounting practices. However, the Atkinsons apparently convinced him to become an active participant in the fraudulent scheme shortly after he joined the company. In addition to continuing the use of the improper accounting methods for the company's video cassettes, the SEC charged the CFO with intentionally failing to record approximately $300,000 of expenses in 1982, a decision which contributed to the material overstatement of The Video Station's reported net income for that year.

In 1988, a federal indictment was filed against the Atkinson brothers. Eventually, George Atkinson pled guilty to submitting false financial information to the SEC and Edward Atkinson was convicted of perjury in connection with the SEC's investigation of The Video Station's financial records. Since the company's CFO was a key government witness against the Atkinson brothers, he was not named in the federal indictment. However, the CFO was sanctioned by the SEC after the federal agency charged him with having engaged in unethical and improper professional conduct.

The Atkinson brothers and the CFO of The Video Station were forced to resign from the company in 1983. The following year, The Video Station filed for protection from its creditors in a federal bankruptcy court. After operating for several months under a court-approved plan of reorganization, the company's assets were sold and it ceased operations. As the degree of competition increased in the video rental industry in the late 1980s and early 1990s, many of The Video Station's former competitors were also forced to discontinue their operations. Contributing to the demise of these companies was the decision of many of the large movie studios to begin selling video cassettes directly to the public thus cutting into the clientele of video rental concerns. Likewise, the revenues of the video rental industry were adversely affected by the increasing availability and utilization of pay-per-view television channels.

QUESTIONS

1. What are the principal differences between a current and noncurrent asset?

2. Why is it important for companies to distinguish between current and noncurrent assets on their periodic balance sheets?

3. What is the purpose of recording depreciation expense on noncurrent assets? Why is it not necessary to depreciate current assets?

4. When the CFO of The Video Station became aware of the company's fraudulent accounting practices, what alternative courses of action were available to him? Identify the parties who were affected by his decision to become involved in the scheme to manipulate the company's reported financial data. What responsibility, if any, did the CFO have to these parties?

5. Assume that a competitor of The Video Station purchased 100,000 videotapes in early 1981 at a total cost of $1,200,000. The company expected the tapes to have a four-year useful life and a salvage value equal to 50 percent of their original cost. The company uses the straight-line method to depreciate its assets. At the end of 1981, the company decided to sell 10,000 of the tapes because they were not generating sufficient rental volume. Similar decisions were made at the end of 1982 and 1983 to sell 50,000 and 30,000 of the tapes, respectively. The company established a selling price for the tapes equal to one-half of their original purchase cost. Prior to placing each block of tapes on sale, the company recorded the proper amount of depreciation expense but did not write the tapes down to the lower of their cost or market value after transferring them from the rental to the sales inventory. Each block of tapes was sold shortly after the beginning of the following fiscal year. For instance, the tapes designated to be sold at the end of 1981 were sold in early 1982. Finally, the 10,000 tapes that the company had on hand at the end of 1984 were sold in early 1985 at their net book value. Determine the total cost of the tapes charged off as an expense or loss each year on this company's 1981–1984 income statements. Also, determine the total cost of the tapes that should have been charged off each year as an expense or loss on the company's 1981–1984 income statements.

Case 3.2
Windmills

The energy conservation policies adopted by President Carter during the late 1970s created widespread interest in alternative or nonfossil fuel sources of energy, including nuclear power, hydropower, and wind power. Significant tax credits and federal subsidies for the wind power industry stimulated dozens of companies to invest significant amounts of capital in research programs designed to develop cost-efficient means to convert one of nature's most abundant resources into a virtually pollution-free form of energy. Unfortunately, most of the early investment ventures in the wind power industry proved to be unprofitable, principally for two reasons. First, many of the early manufacturers of windmills and windmill replacement parts failed to test thoroughly their products before marketing them.

As a result, the first generation of commercially available windmills suffered from a high rate of technical failure. Second, the worldwide drop in oil prices in the early 1980s curtailed the federal government's interest in subsidizing research and development activities relating to wind power. In fact, the Reagan Administration allowed most of President Carter's incentive programs for investment in the wind power industry to expire during the mid–1980s.

In 1978, Pro–Mation, Inc., a small, privately held corporation headquartered in Jamestown, New York, began exploring potential investment opportunities in the wind power industry. The following year, the stockholders of Pro–Mation established Energy Collectors, Inc., a company whose sole purpose was to engage in wind power research and development activities. For its entire existence, Energy Collectors was dependent upon Pro–Mation to fund its operations since the company produced only modest revenues compared to its sizable research and development expenditures. The following table documents the increasingly poor operating results of Energy Collectors from 1980 through 1983.

Year Ended [1]	Revenues	Costs and Expenses	Net Operating Loss
3/31/80	$ 3,900	$ 83,870	($ 79,970)
3/31/81	$48,200	$ 86,650	($ 38,450)
3/31/82	$28,209	$175,331	($147,122)
3/31/83	$29,500	$201,050	($171,550)

---

1. The information in this table and all subsequent quotes was taken from Accounting and Auditing Enforcement Release No. 71, issued August 29, 1985, by the Securities and Exchange Commission.

Pro-Mation recorded transfers of funds to Energy Collectors by debiting a receivable account and crediting cash. By March 31, 1983, the total balance of the receivable from Energy Collectors had reached $321,725. Pro–Mation also recorded periodic interest income on the receivable from Energy Collectors. However, Energy Collectors never actually paid any interest on the large debt it owed to Pro–Mation. Instead, Pro–Mation's accountants simply added the unpaid interest charges to the balance of the receivable.

In September 1983, Pro–Mation filed a registration statement with the Securities and Exchange Commission (SEC) for the purpose of selling stock to the general public. As required by federal securities laws, Pro–Mation's registration statement contained a set of financial statements audited by the company's accounting firm. These financial statements, which were for the 1981 through 1983 fiscal years of Pro–Mation, included the large receivable due from Energy Collectors. As shown by the following table, the receivable from Energy Collectors accounted for a significant portion of the total net assets of Pro–Mation during the early 1980s.

Balance Sheet Date	Receivable Due From Energy Collectors	Stockholders' Equity (Net Assets)
3/31/81	$108,434	$175,201
3/31/82	$208,146	$271,367
3/31/83	$321,725	$403,391

The interest income recorded on the receivable due from Energy Collectors also represented a significant portion of Pro–Mation's reported profits for the period 1981 through 1983, accounting for as much as 20 percent of the company's net income during that time frame. After reviewing Pro–Mation's registration statement, the SEC maintained that the document misled investors when it reported that the company had "realized" interest income on the receivable due from Energy Collectors.

> The use of the word "realized" is misleading in light of the fact that the interest accrued was never actually received, but rather was added to the account receivable and remained subject to the risk of uncollectability.

In March 1984, the SEC suspended Pro–Mation's registration statement, effectively preventing the company from selling its common stock to the public. The SEC alleged that Pro–Mation had inappropriately accounted for the receivable from Energy Collectors. More specifically, the SEC charged that Pro–Mation's accountants should have reduced the receivable to its net realizable value rather than listing it on the company's year-end balance sheets as simply the sum total of the loans made to Energy Collectors plus the accrued but unpaid interest income.

In criticizing Pro–Mation's accounting for the receivable from Energy Collectors, the SEC referred to Financial Accounting Standard (FAS) No. 5, *Accounting for Contingencies*. The SEC pointed out that FAS No. 5 requires entities in such circumstances to record a loss when two conditions are met: 1) available information suggests that the value of an asset has been impaired, and 2) the amount of the loss can be reasonably estimated. The SEC concluded that Pro–Mation's executives should have recognized that both of these conditions were met when the company prepared the registration statement in September 1983 since Energy Collectors' "earnings prospects for the foreseeable future were minimal because it had been unsuccessful in its attempts to market its products." As a result, the SEC ruled that Pro–Mation should have recorded a loss equal to the full amount of the receivable due from Energy Collectors and reported the receivable on its year-end balance sheets at a nominal value of $1.

Pro–Mation's executives were not the only parties criticized by the SEC for the improper accounting for the large receivable from Energy Collectors. The accounting firm that audited the financial statements of Pro–Mation included in the company's 1983 registration statement was also severely chastised by the federal agency. According to the SEC, the accounting firm should have known that it was inappropriate to allow Pro–Mation to carry the receivable from Energy Collectors at its face value on the company's year-end balance sheets.

> [Pro–Mation's independent accountants] knew of Energy Collectors' growing financial difficulties. Consequently, they also knew, or should have known, that Pro–Mation failed to present its Form S–1 financial statements in accordance with generally accepted accounting principles by not writing down its investment in Energy Collectors to net realizable value.

In fact, the SEC's review of the audit workpapers of Pro-Mation's accounting firm disclosed that members of that firm had been concerned by the potential overstatement of the receivable from Energy Collectors.

Nevertheless, the accounting firm chose not to ask Pro–Mation's management to adjust that account balance. The justification given for this decision in the audit workpapers was that the net realizable value of the receivable from Energy Collectors could not be determined. That is, the accounting firm maintained that the second condition identified by FAS No. 5 for recording a loss in such circumstances was not satisfied.

Pro–Mation filed for protection from its creditors under the federal bankruptcy laws in 1984 shortly after the SEC initiated its investigation into the company's accounting for the large receivable due from Energy Collectors. In August 1985, the SEC ordered the accounting firm that had audited Pro–Mation's annual financial statements to implement a system of controls to improve the quality of its professional audit services. In addition, the SEC suspended the accounting firm's right to practice before it for a period of one year.

On the bright side, the wind power industry eventually rebounded from the troubling times it experienced in the early 1980s. By 1990, technological breakthroughs in the industry had reduced the per megawatt cost to produce wind power to a level essentially equivalent to that of the per megawatt production cost of electricity generated by fossil fuels. Although wind power will likely never become a primary source of electricity because of its dependence upon the whim of Mother Nature, it is projected to become a very important secondary source of energy by the second decade of the 21st century, quite possibly generating more electricity than either nuclear or hydropower sources.

QUESTIONS

1. How, if at all, did Pro–Mation benefit by recording interest income on the receivable due from Energy Collectors?

2. Accountants often refer to the "realization principle." Define that principle. In your view, did Pro–Mation violate the realization principle when it recorded interest income on the receivable from Energy Collectors? Explain.

3. For balance sheet purposes, most assets are reported at historical cost, which was the valuation basis used by Pro–Mation to report its investment in Energy Collectors. Identify some of the limitations of using historical costs for balance sheet reporting purposes.

4. The SEC ruled that the investment in (receivable from) Energy Collectors should have been accounted for at its net realizable value by Pro–Mation. Identify the principal limitations of using net realizable values as the primary basis for reporting assets on entities' balance sheets.

5. Other than historical cost and net realizable value, what valuation bases could be used for balance sheet reporting purposes for assets? Briefly identify the principal advantages and disadvantages of utilizing these valuation bases.

6. Companies which intend to sell stock on an interstate basis are required by federal securities laws to file a registration statement with the SEC before the stock can be marketed. Subsequently, such companies must file annual financial reports with the SEC. What is the principal regulatory function of the SEC?

7.   Why are companies required to have the financial statements which they include in registration statements and the annual financial reports which they file with the SEC audited by an independent accounting firm?

8.   The financial statement footnotes of many publicly owned companies include a discussion of contingencies for which losses have not been recorded. Identify footnotes describing loss contingencies in recent annual reports of three publicly owned companies. In each case, summarize the nature of the contingency and explain why the company believed that recording a loss for that contingency was not necessary. Why does FAS No. 5 require companies to disclose unrecorded loss contingencies in their financial statement footnotes?

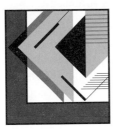

CASE 3.3
POOLS, PUDDLES, AND
INVENTORY ACCOUNTING

Inventory is typically the most important asset of companies engaged in merchandising or manufacturing. Failure of an entity to manage properly its investment in inventory may result in disrupted production schedules, dissatisfied customers, as well as significant losses due to inventory obsolescence and theft. From an accounting standpoint, errors in the inventory account have significant implications for both an entity's income statement and its balance sheet. Consequently, accounting decisions that affect a company's inventory balance must be carefully considered.

Most inventory accounting issues are related to valuation concerns. One of the first accounting decisions that must be made for inventory is which costs to include in the inventory account. Generally accepted accounting principles (GAAP) dictate that only certain costs related to inventory can be treated as inventoriable or product costs. Inventoriable costs are not recorded immediately as expenses on an entity's income statement but instead are charged to the inventory account and then subsequently recognized as cost of goods sold when the items to which the costs are attached are sold. For instance, in a manufacturing setting, the principal materials used in the production process are always considered product costs. Conversely, expenses incurred to market a product, such as advertising expenditures and sales commissions, are treated as "period" costs and thus expensed in the period incurred.

Another important inventory accounting decision is the choice of a cost flow assumption. Companies that sell relatively expensive products, such as televisions, refrigerators, automobiles, etc., maintain detailed accounting records that allow them to determine the exact cost of the items sold during any given accounting period. However, the maintenance of elaborate inventory records is usually not cost-effective when a company sells a high volume of relatively inexpensive products. Likewise, manufacturing concerns generally cannot justify maintaining inventory records that would allow them to identify the actual costs of the materials used in a production process during any given period. In these latter contexts, companies adopt a cost flow assumption, such as first-in, first-out (FIFO), or last-in, first-out (LIFO), to use in tracking inventory costs as they flow through the accounting records. GAAP does not require that the cost flow assumption adopted by a company correspond with the actual physical flow of goods. For instance, even though goods flow through a company's operations on a FIFO basis, the entity can still elect to adopt the LIFO cost flow assumption for accounting purposes.

The ease with which an entity's operating results can be distorted by manipulating the inventory account entices companies, particularly companies in financial distress, to misstate the period-ending balance of their inventory account or accounts. In 1984, the Securities and Exchange Commission (SEC) charged that Stauffer Chemical Company, a large, Connecticut-based firm whose principal line of business is the manufacture and sale of agricultural chemicals, had intentionally misrepresented its 1982 year-end inventory balance to conceal its poor operating results for that year.[1]

During the early 1980s, Stauffer's profitability was adversely affected by a series of uncontrollable circumstances. First, three consecutive years of rainy spring weather in the midwestern United States cut sharply into the sales of Stauffer's principal product, a corn herbicide designed to work most effectively in dry soil. Second, a federal program designed to encourage farmers to reduce their production levels lowered the demand for several of Stauffer's fertilizers and herbicides. Finally, Stauffer was forced to lower

---

1. Most of the background material for this case and all the quotes included in it were taken from Accounting and Auditing Enforcement Release No. 35, issued August 13, 1984, by the Securities and Exchange Commission.

the price of one of its primary products to be more competitive with a new product introduced by another chemical company.

The SEC charged that Stauffer executives attempted to counteract the negative impact of these three circumstances on the company's net income for 1982 by utilizing a number of questionable methods that both increased the firm's reported sales for that year and understated the firm's year-end inventory balances, thereby inflating its gross profit. One such method involved the company's "Early Order Program" (EOP) which had been established several years earlier. Under this program, distributors of Stauffer's products routinely ordered inventory in the last few months of one year that was intended to be sold during the first quarter of the following year. A key stipulation of the program was that Stauffer's distributors would not be billed for EOP orders until the first quarter of the following year. In late fiscal 1982, however, Stauffer added economic incentives to the program to induce its distributors to allow EOP orders to be billed to them during the fourth quarter of 1982 rather than during the first quarter of 1983. The economic incentives proved successful as Stauffer's revenues and profits increased sharply in the final quarter of 1982. Unfortunately, a lower than expected demand for Stauffer's products in the spring of 1983 forced the company to repurchase a large percentage of the product shipped to its distributors in the fourth quarter of the previous year.[2]

2. Stauffer voluntarily offered to repurchase the excess amounts of product from its customers to maintain good relations with them.

The most clever of the methods used by Stauffer executives to manipulate the company's 1982 year-end inventory balances and operating results involved a modification of the LIFO inventory method. When a company adopts the LIFO cost flow assumption, the inventory sold or used in a production process during a given period is assumed to have been taken from the most recently acquired inventory items. For instance, assume that Exhibit 1 illustrates the activity in two inventory accounts during fiscal 1994. Using the LIFO method, the 3,000 pounds of Mix1 inventory on December 31, 1994, would be valued at $55,000, while the 4,000 pounds of Mix2 on that date would be valued at $8,000.[3] Alternatively, under the FIFO cost flow assumption, the 1994 ending inventory of Mix1 would be priced at $25 per pound for a collective value of $75,000, while the ending inventory of Mix2 would be valued at $18,000 (3,000 pounds at $5 each and 1,000 pounds at $3 each).

In recent years, many companies have adopted the LIFO method for taxation purposes since in a period of steadily increasing prices it permits them to reduce their taxable income and, consequently, their tax liabilities. However, if a company adopts the LIFO method for taxation purposes, it must use LIFO for financial reporting purposes as well. As a result, the adoption of the LIFO cost flow assumption typically

---

3. The situation illustrated in Exhibit 1 assumes that the company in question used a periodic rather than perpetual inventory system. If a perpetual inventory system had been used, it would have been necessary to identify the actual dates of the sales transactions and the amount of product sold in each transaction to compute the proper dollar value of the ending inventory balance.

Exhibit 1 Illustration of LIFO Method

Item: Mix1

Beginning Inventory, January 1, 1994	1,000 pounds @ $15	$15,000
Purchases:		
March 1	2,000 pounds @ $20	
October 15	3,000 pounds @ $25	
Sales:		
January 1—December 31	3,000 pounds	
Ending Inventory, December 31, 1994	1,000 pounds @ $15	
	2,000 pounds @ $20	$55,000

Item: Mix2

Beginning Inventory, January 1, 1994	4,000 pounds @ $2	$8,000
Purchases:		
June 10	2,000 pounds @ $3	
November 25	3,000 pounds @ $5	
Sales:		
January 1—December 31	5,000 pounds	
Ending Inventory, December 31, 1994	4,000 pounds @ $2	$8,000

results in not only lower taxes for a company but lower reported profits on its periodic income statements as well.

Since 1974, Stauffer had been using a modified version of the LIFO method known as the LIFO pooling method. The LIFO pooling method allows companies to apply the LIFO cost flow assumption to "pools" of substantially identical inventory items rather than using the much more cumbersome approach of applying the LIFO cost flow assumption to each individual inventory item. For instance, a company, such as Stauffer, that sells a large number of agricultural fertilizers is permitted to apply the LIFO method to "pools" of fertilizers that are very similar rather than being required to apply the method to each individual type of fertilizer.

To illustrate the LIFO pooling method, assume that an inventory pool consisting of the two products shown in Exhibit 1 (Mix1 and Mix2) was created at the beginning of 1994. The January 1, 1994, balance of this new inventory pool would be $23,000, the sum of the values of the two previously separate account balances. Exhibit 2 illustrates how the LIFO pooling method would be applied to the Mix1–Mix2 inventory pool during 1994. At the end of 1994, the physical quantity of the goods included in the pool would be priced out using the LIFO method, but no effort would be made to ascertain the actual quantities of the specific products in the pool on hand at the end of the period. Instead, the LIFO assumption would simply be applied on a "blind" basis to the ending inventory quantities. (Notice that the ending inventory value of the Mix1–Mix2 inventory pool is equal to the sum of the ending balances of the Mix1 and Mix2 accounts under the assumption that they were maintained separately as shown in Exhibit 1. Typically, this will not be the case.)

In 1974, Stauffer defined eight inventory pools for the purpose of applying the LIFO pooling method. However, in 1982, when Stauffer was facing signifi-

---

Exhibit 2 Illustration of LIFO Pooling Method

Inventory Pool: Mix1–Mix2

Beginning Inventory, January 1, 1994	5,000 pounds @ $ 4.60	$23,000
Purchases:		
March 1	2,000 pounds @ $20	
June 10	2,000 pounds @ $3	
October 15	3,000 pounds @ $25	
November 25	3,000 pounds @ $5	
Sales:		
January 1— December 31	8,000 pounds	
Ending Inventory, December 31, 1994	5,000 pounds @ $ 4.60	
	2,000 pounds @ $20	$63,000

cant economic problems, its management decided to segregate the eight inventory pools into 280 inventory "puddles." By opportunistically defining these puddles, Stauffer management was able to liquidate a significant portion of its inventory at low per unit prices, resulting, of course, in a significant increase in reported profits—as well as income taxes.

Stauffer's LIFO puddle implementation process began in the spring of 1982. As puddles were proposed, the impact on earnings resulting from each proposed change was calculated by Stauffer accounting personnel. Stauffer evaluated a series of three company-wide LIFO puddle proposals. On each of these three occasions, Stauffer increased the potential earnings from anticipated LIFO liquidations.

To illustrate how Stauffer's "puddling" scheme could be used to increase a company's reported profits, refer to Exhibit 2. Assume that the company in this illustration forecast that its customers would purchase only 3,000 pounds of product from the Mix1–Mix2 inventory pool the following year, 1995. (Recall that the products grouped together in an inventory pool should be substantially identical. For purposes of this illustration, assume that Mix1 and Mix2 are interchangeable.) Consequently, the company budgeted no additional purchases of either Mix1 or Mix2 during 1995. If the pool shown in Exhibit 2 was left intact, the cost of goods sold for 1995 for this pool would be $44,600: 2,000 pounds @ $20 each and 1,000 pounds @ $4.60 each.

Conversely, assume that the actual physical flow of goods for the two products for 1994 is depicted by Exhibit 1. Also assume that the inventory pool shown in Exhibit 2 is split into two "puddles" at the beginning of 1995, one containing the 3,000 pounds of Mix1 and the other containing the 4,000 pounds of Mix2. If the company chooses to allocate the $63,000 inventory value to the new two puddles by using the data in Exhibit 1, the Mix1 puddle will be allocated a value of $55,000 at the beginning of 1995, while the Mix2 puddle will be allocated a value of $8,000. Given this new puddle structure, the company could choose to allot all 3,000 pounds of 1995's sales to the Mix2 account, resulting in a cost-of-goods-sold of only $6,000 for that year versus a $44,600 cost-of-goods-sold that would have been recognized if the inventory pool structure had been retained. Of course, the lower cost-of-goods-sold figure would effectively increase the company's gross profit and pre-tax profit by $38,600.

The cumulative effect of Stauffer's inventory manipulation scheme on its 1982 net income was an overstatement of more than 25 percent, in dollar terms $31.1 million. The SEC alleged that this error was sufficiently large to cause Stauffer's financial statements to be materially misleading to the investing and lending public. Eventually, Stauffer executives settled the charges brought against them and their company by the SEC by agreeing to issue revised financial statements for 1982.

QUESTIONS

1. In tabular form, indicate how the following financial statement items are affected when a company overstates its period-ending inventory: cost of goods sold, income tax expense, current assets, retained earnings. How would each of these items be affected, if at all, in the following accounting period?

2. In a period of deflation, identify the cost flow assumption, LIFO or FIFO, that companies would prefer to use for (a) financial reporting purposes, (b) taxation purposes. Explain.

3. Should companies be allowed to change the accounting methods they apply from one period to the next simply to improve their reported operating results? In your opinion, under what general conditions or circumstances should companies be allowed to change their accounting methods?

4. Prior to 1982, Stauffer shipped goods to its customers under its early order program (EOP) during the fourth quarter of a fiscal year but waited until the first quarter of the following year to "book" these shipments as sales. Identify the general conditions which should be met before a sales transaction is recorded. Was it appropriate for Stauffer to delay recording EOP shipments as sales until the first quarter of the following fiscal year? Explain.

5. The efforts by Stauffer management in fiscal 1982 to increase the company's profits for financial reporting purposes also resulted in the company having a higher taxable income. What was the net economic effect on Stauffer of the efforts by its executives to increase its reported profits? In your view, were the actions of Stauffer's executives "rational"?

6. Research the **Wall Street Journal** or other business publications and identify three cases in recent years in which the ending inventory balance of a company was intentionally overstated. For each of these cases, record the following information: the entity involved, the specific methods used to overstate inventory, the impact on the entity's reported operating results and apparent financial condition, and the consequences for the company and the individuals who were responsible for overstating the inventory balance.

7. Assume that you are a CPA and have been retained as a financial consultant by the owner of a small manufacturing company. This individual has asked you to write a report to him describing accounting "gimmicks" and other methods that can be used to inflate reported profits by manipulating the year-end balance of inventory. Apparently, this individual wants to use such methods for his company. Write an appropriate report or memorandum to the owner regarding this initial assignment.

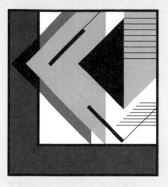

FULL AND FAIR DISCLOSURE

Section Four

Fundamental Concepts of Accounting

Clearly, the stockholders and creditors of Great American had the right to a more complete and honest set of financial statements than those provided to them by the company's executives. However, in most cases, determining exactly how much information stockholders, creditors, and other parties are entitled to receive is much more difficult. Consider two cases. During the 1970s, were the individuals relying on the financial statements of Mattel, Inc., entitled to know that the toy manufacturer had a huge and apparently unsalable inventory of "Hot Wheels" that had piled up in its warehouses due to a sudden change in children's taste for that toy? Probably. During the same time frame, were third parties entitled to know that Ruth Handler, one of Mattel's co-founders and the person largely responsible for the company's financial success, had been diagnosed with a life-threatening disease? Probably not.

THE SEC: CARETAKER OF THE PUBLIC INTEREST

Since the passage of the federal securities laws of the early 1930s, the authority to regulate the financial reporting practices of publicly owned companies whose stock is sold on an interstate basis has been vested with the Securities and Exchange Commission (SEC). Prior to the passage of the Securities Act of 1933 and the Securities Exchange Act of 1934, flim-flam men and con artists fleeced honest investors almost at will. In fact, in the decade that preceded the 1929 collapse of the United States stock market more

than $50 billion of corporate securities were pur-
chased by the general public, at least one-half of
which were worthless or essentially worthless at the
time they were sold.[1]

To restore credibility to the nation's stock market
and to protect investors from fraudulent investment
schemes, Congress was forced to impose rigorous financial disclosure rules on publicly owned companies. Congress's primary intent in establishing the
SEC was to ensure that investors, creditors, and other
interested parties were provided with "full and fair
disclosure" regarding the financial affairs of publicly
owned companies. When it adopted the federal securities laws, Congress never intended to prohibit the
sale of highly speculative securities. Consequently, the
SEC does not attempt to assess the investment quality
of new securities but rather is simply charged with
ensuring that all relevant information regarding the
securities and the companies issuing them is provided
to the investing and lending public.

Determining exactly what constitutes full and fair
disclosure has been an issue that the SEC has wres-
tled with for decades. In the early days of the federal
agency, its first commissioner, Joseph Kennedy, Sr.,
relied heavily on the public accounting profession to
dictate the content of publicly released financial statements. Since that time, the SEC has generally allowed
the private rule-making bodies within the accounting
profession, such as the Financial Accounting Standards Board (FASB) and the Auditing Standards

---

1. K.F. Skousen, *An Introduction to the SEC* (Cincinnati:
South–Western Publishing, 1980): 5.

Board (ASB), to determine the form and content of publicly released financial statements.

FUNDAMENTALS OF FINANCIAL DISCLOSURE

In 1978, the FASB began issuing a series of Statements on Financial Accounting Concepts (SFACs) to define the fundamental elements and concepts of financial accounting and financial reporting practices. Among the more important issues addressed by SFACs are the primary objectives of financial reporting, the question of to whom financial statements should be addressed, the key characteristics that publicly released financial data should possess, and the principal constraints on published financial data.

According to SFAC No. 1, *Objectives of Financial Reporting by Business Enterprises*, the principal purpose of financial reporting should be to "provide information that is useful in making business and economic decisions—for making reasoned choices among alternative uses of scarce resources in the conduct of business and economic activities." [2] SFAC No. 1 goes on to state that the information which best facilitates the economic decisions of financial statement users is information concerning a given entity's future cash flow prospects.

> People engage in investing, lending, and similar activities primarily to increase their cash resources. The ultimate

---

2. "Objectives of Financial Reporting by Business Enterprises," *Statement of Financial Accounting Concepts No. 1* (New York: AICPA, 1978): para. 9.

test of success (or failure) of those activities is the extent to which they return more or (less) cash than they
cost.[3]

For many years, the accounting profession debated
the question of to which general class of financial
statement users financial reports should be addressed.
Many parties within the profession expressed the
view that financial reports should be understandable
by the general public, including individuals who are
relatively naive about financial reporting and accounting issues. Conversely, other parties maintained that
financial reports should be prepared under the assumption that users have an in-depth understanding
of financial reporting and accounting issues. SFAC
No. 1 settled this debate by concluding that financial
reports should be comprehensible to individuals who
have a "reasonable understanding of business and economic activities" and are willing to "study the information with reasonable diligence." [4]

The purpose of SFAC No. 2, *Qualitative Characteristics of Accounting Information*, is to define the most
important attributes that financial statement data
should possess. According to SFAC No. 2, relevance
and reliability are the two indispensable characteristics of accounting information. If either of these two
attributes are absent in a given set of accounting data,
that data will be of no use to financial decision makers.

For data to be relevant, it must first be timely. If
information is provided too late to influence financial

---

3. Ibid., para. 38.

4. Ibid., para. 34.

statement users' decisions, then, by definition, it is not relevant to those decisions. In addition to timeliness, accounting data must have predictive value, and/or feedback value in order to satisfy the relevance requirement according to SFAC No. 2. That is, accounting data should be useful in predicting an entity's future cash flows or it should allow users "to confirm or correct earlier expectations" regarding an entity's cash flows.[5]

SFAC No. 2 notes that to be reliable, accounting data should possess the following traits: verifiability, neutrality, and representational faithfulness. Accounting data does not have to be subject to precise quantification to qualify as verifiable. In fact, SFAC No. 1 notes that most financial data are not subject to precise quantification.

> . . . despite the aura of precision that may seem to surround financial reporting in general and financial statements in particular, with few exceptions the measures are approximations, which may be based on rules and convention, rather than exact amounts.[6]

Instead of implying mathematical precision, the term verifiability suggests that a group of professional accountants should be able to reach some degree of consensus regarding the appropriate measurement to be assigned to a given financial statement item. As an

---

5. "Qualitative Characteristics of Accounting Information." *Statement of Financial Accounting Concepts No. 2* (New York: AICPA, 1980): para. 51.

6. "Objectives of Financial Reporting by Business Enterprises," para. 20.

example, if several accountants arrived at fairly close approximations of a company's allowance for uncollectible receivables, that allowance would satisfy the verifiability requirement.

To qualify as neutral, accounting data must be presented without "bias towards a predetermined result" according to SFAC No. 2.[7] That is, preparers of accounting data should not consciously attempt to influence the decisions of the users of accounting data. To use a cliche, accountants should not have a hidden agenda when presenting data to financial statement users. If accountants chose to present data in such a way as to achieve some desired outcome, eventually the accountants themselves and the data they provide would lose credibility and, consequently, their usefulness to financial decision makers.

The term "representational faithfulness" implies that accounting data should portray the underlying events, economic resources, and obligations that it is intended to portray. As an example, E.F. Hutton & Co., at one point the second largest brokerage firm in the nation, was criticized by a congressional investigative committee during the 1980s for failing to adequately disclose in its annual financial statements that it had overdrawn its bank accounts by huge amounts. Instead of referring to these amounts as "Cash Overdrafts" in the liability section of its balance sheet, the brokerage firm instead used the less definitive, and possibly misleading, phrase "Drafts and Checks Pay-

---

7. "Qualitative Characteristics of Accounting Information," para. 99.

able." Because of this lack of clarity, Hutton's financial statements failed to represent faithfully the nature of the firm's very poor cash position.

SFAC No. 2 notes that, in certain circumstances, it is not feasible or necessary for accounting data to satisfy the relevance and reliability requirements. For instance, accountants do not have to ensure that accounting data is perfectly reliable if the imprecision in that data would not be sufficiently large to "matter" to financial statement users. An important litigation case involving an accounting firm illustrated this point very clearly.[8] The presiding judge in that case ruled that even though the earnings of the company in question were overstated, the overstatement was not large enough to affect the decisions of the individuals relying on the company's financial statements. "Materiality" is the term that accountants use when referring to the relative importance of financial statement items. By definition, immaterial items or amounts are not important enough to influence financial statement users' decisions.

Finally, accountants should weigh the relative costs and benefits of ensuring that a given set of accounting data is relevant and reliable. That is, it would not be reasonable to require reporting entities to ensure that their accounting data are relevant and reliable at any cost. At some point, the incremental cost of providing more relevant and reliable accounting data exceeds the incremental benefit.

---

8. Escott v. BarChris Construction Corporation, 283 F.Supp. 643 (1968).

ROADBLOCKS TO IMPLEMENTATION OF FINANCIAL DISCLOSURE RULES

In addition to the broad, conceptual guidelines regarding financial disclosure, rule-making bodies in the accounting profession have issued a large number of specific disclosure rules that apply to marketable securities, leases, inventory, income taxes, and dozens of other financial statement items. In spite of these extensive and detailed disclosure rules, critics of the rule-making bodies in the accounting profession contend that the users of financial statements often do not receive sufficient information or sufficiently concise and coherent information to make fully informed economic decisions. One of the major problems that decision makers encounter when they use externally reported accounting data is a lack of uniformity by reporting entities in interpreting and applying financial disclosure rules. This lack of uniformity is not necessarily the fault of the accountants who prepare financial statements, but more often is attributable to the underlying subjectivity of many financial disclosure rules.

As an example, Financial Accounting Standard (FAS) No. 5, *Accounting for Contingencies*, requires accountants to assess the likelihood that a loss contingency, such as a pending lawsuit, will result in an actual loss eventually being incurred by a given entity. In making this assessment, accountants must determine whether the likelihood of an actual loss is "remote," "reasonably possible," or "probable." Surprisingly, FAS No. 5 does not provide any explicit guidelines regarding the level of probability or likelihood that should be associated with each of these terms. The accountant's assessment of the likelihood of a loss contingency becoming an actual loss is critical since that assessment largely determines whether and/or how the item will be disclosed in the financial statements. As might be expected, research studies of FAS No. 5 decisions have found significant variance in how accountants interpret the terms "remote," "reasonably possible," and "probable." [9] Consequently, financial statement users receive differing opinions regarding the likelihood of unfavorable outcomes to loss contingencies simply because accountants do not interpret the disclosure rules of FAS No. 5 uniformly.

Another factor that adversely affects the implementation of financial disclosure rules is the economic self-interest of reporting entities. As one corporate executive noted, most companies tend to have "an innate fear of disclosure." [10] This fear often stems from concern that information disclosed publicly will be used by competitors. The cost of accumulating and presenting financial data also serves to discourage companies from complying fully with financial disclosure rules.

In recent years, one of the most heated controversies involving the failure of companies to comply with financial disclosure rules centered on the auditor change disclosure rules of the SEC. The Securities Exchange Act of 1934 requires publicly owned compa-

---

9. J. Jiambalvo and N. Wilner, "Auditor Evaluation of Contingent Claims," *Auditing: A Journal of Practice and Theory*, vol. 5 (Fall 1985): 1–11.

10. D. Weschler and K. Wandyez, "An Innate Fear of Disclosure," *Forbes* (February 5, 1990): 76, 78.

nies to have their periodic financial statements audited by independent accounting firms. These audits are essential because they help ensure that public companies issue materially accurate financial statements, thus enhancing the credibility of these financial statements for investors, creditors, and other user groups who do not have access to the financial records of reporting entities.

Prior to 1970, public companies and their accounting firms typically had long and stable relationships with changes in accounting firms being made only under unusual circumstances, such as a corporate merger. However, the rate of accounting firm dismissals increased dramatically in the 1970s. One explanation for this phenomenon was that companies were firing their accounting firms when they anticipated receiving an unfavorable audit opinion on their financial statements. Allegedly, such companies would then "shop" for another accounting firm that would issue a more desirable opinion on their financial statements. As a direct result of these opinion shopping allegations, the SEC adopted a set of rules requiring public companies to disclose the circumstances surrounding auditor changes. For instance, companies that change accounting firms are required to disclose, in a publicly available document, whether they had any serious disagreements with their former accounting firm concerning technical accounting or auditing issues. The purpose of such disclosures is to allow financial statement users to decide what motivated specific companies to dismiss their accounting firms.

Unfortunately, the SEC's disclosure rules regarding changes in accounting firms have been ineffective to a large degree. In most cases, an auditor change announcement provides few insights into the contextual circumstances that precipitated the change. For instance, relatively few of these announcements have disclosed that technical disagreements preceded changes in auditors; although subsequent research of SEC enforcement cases and litigation cases spawned by auditor changes suggests that such disagreements are quite common.[11] Most likely, auditor change disclosure rules are relatively ineffective because companies engaging in opinion shopping behavior have an incentive to conceal that fact from the general public. Since it is very difficult for the SEC to prove after the fact that disclosures regarding an auditor change were less than candid, a company that switches auditors for an illicit reason may subvert the disclosure rules by providing only minimal information in its auditor change announcement.

On occasion, public companies abuse financial disclosure rules by disclosing too much rather than too little information. Such was the case with Prepaid Legal Services, Inc., a small publicly owned company headquartered in Ada, Oklahoma. In 1983 and 1984, Prepaid reported the earnings per share figures shown below.

	Fiscal Year Ending December 31,	
	1983	1984
Primary Earnings per Share	($.02)	$.00
Fully Diluted Earnings per Share	$.05	$.12

---

11. M.C. Knapp and F.M. Elikai, "Auditor Changes and Information Suppression," *Research in Accounting Regulation*, vol. 4 (1990): 3–20.

Fully diluted earnings per share is essentially a company's earnings per share in a worst case scenario. That is, if a company has common stock equivalents outstanding, such as, preferred stock that is convertible into common stock, the company is required to compute two earnings per share figures: its actual or primary earnings per share and the earnings per share it would have earned if the common stock equivalents had been converted into common stock. However, there is an important exception to this rule. If the assumed conversion of any common stock equivalents would result in an increase in the reported earnings per share, then the fully diluted earnings per share should not be presented.

Prepaid disclosed both primary and fully diluted earnings per share figures in 1983 and 1984 even though its fully diluted earnings per share was greater than its primary earnings per share. In justifying this decision, Prepaid reported in its annual financial statements that "Management believes the [fully diluted earnings per share] calculation presents a more historic, consistent and meaningful view of earnings per share." [12] However, the SEC did not agree with the reasoning of Prepaid's management. After publicly scolding the company, the federal agency required Prepaid's officials to amend the previously issued financial statements that contained the inappropriate earnings per share figures.

---

12. *Accounting and Auditing Enforcement Release No. 121.* Securities and Exchange Commission (Washington, D.C.: U.S. Government Printing Office, 1986).

QUESTIONS

1. How could the race horse owned by Great American Financial, Inc., be recorded on the company's balance sheet at a value of $550,000 when just a few months earlier it had been offered for sale at a price of $5,000 by the individual who owned the horse at that time? Explain.

2. Identify the parties to whom corporate management has a responsibility to provide honest and complete information regarding its company's financial affairs. How would each of these parties be affected by incomplete and/or inaccurate financial information?

3. This case notes that Mattel, Inc., the toy manufacturer, accumulated a large inventory of Hot Wheels toys during the early 1970s due to a sudden drop in demand for that toy. Assume that the inventory of that item had cost Mattel $5,000,000 to produce and that the company could have realized $500,000 from "scrapping" the toys. Also assume that the toys could have been sold to discount retailers for $1,000,000. However, Mattel typically did not sell to discount retailers because these companies were perceived by the public to sell inferior products. Which alternative method of disposing of the Hot Wheels toys should Mattel have chosen given the facts provided? Prior to disposing of these toys, at what value should Mattel have reported them on its balance sheet?

4. Provide a numerical example that demonstrates how the fully diluted earnings per share of Prepaid

Legal Services, Inc., could have been greater than its primary earnings per share. Assume in your example that the company's only common stock equivalent was outstanding bonds payable that were convertible into common stock.

5. According to the FASB, externally prepared financial statements should be addressed to relatively sophisticated financial statement users. What implications does this position have for naive or unsophisticated financial statement users? Explain why you believe the FASB adopted this position.

6. For the following asset accounts, identify and briefly discuss problems that accountants likely experience in ensuring that the financial statement amounts reported for each of the accounts is "reliable": cash, inventory, marketable securities, and buildings. (Note: In your response, you will likely want to refer to verifiability, neutrality, and representational faithfulness, the three key traits of reliablity in this context.)

7. Obtain and record the total sales, total assets, and net income figures for the three most recent fiscal years of four public companies that have major operations in your state or community. For each company, identify the minimum amount for each year that, in your opinion, would qualify as "material" to the individuals who use and rely upon the financial statements of these companies. That is, what is the minimum overstatement in each net income amount that would be sufficiently large to affect the decisions of financial statement users? Justify your choice in each case. In your opinion, which type of financial statement users, stockholders or creditors, would be most concerned with a material overstatement of a company's net income? Explain.

8. Assume that a long-time friend of yours who is now a practicing attorney has recently been retained by a stockholder of a company to file suit against the company for issuing materially misstated financial statements. Your friend is confused by the concept of materiality and has asked you to write a brief report, for which he will compensate you, describing in laymen's terms the concept of materiality. He would also like you to use concrete examples in your report. Draft such a report using the data you collected for the prior question as the source of the examples that the attorney wants included in the report.

CASE 4.2
ONCE UPON A TIME ON A BALANCE SHEET: HISTORICAL COSTS VS. CURRENT VALUES

Clabir Corporation was founded in 1972 in Old Greenwich, Connecticut, and reorganized as a holding company eight years later. Following its reorganization, Clabir's principal assets were controlling interests in two publicly owned companies, The Isaly Company and General Defense Corporation. At the time, Isaly's principal operations involved the production and sale of the popular "Klondike" ice cream bar, while General Defense was a leading supplier of tank ammunition to the United States Army and several countries allied with the United States. In late 1980, Clabir began acquiring stock in U.S. Industries,

Inc. (USI), a conglomerate. Eventually, Clabir would acquire nearly 10 percent of the outstanding common stock of USI, an investment which represented approximately 30 percent of Clabir's total assets. The table below discloses the aggregate cost and market value of the investment in USI stock at the end of each quarter of Clabir's 1982 fiscal year which ended January 31, 1982.

Date	Aggregate Cost	Aggregate Market Value
4/30/81	$17,931,679	$16,846,170
7/31/81	17,931,679	22,227,411
10/31/81	23,494,623	21,429,000
1/31/82	24,508,102	21,131,375

Financial Accounting Standard (FAS) No. 12, *Accounting for Certain Marketable Securities*, requires companies to report short-term investments in marketable securities at the lower of cost or market value in their periodic balance sheets. Consequently, Clabir's April 30, 1981, balance sheet filed with the Securities and Exchange Commission (SEC) listed the investment in USI stock at its aggregate market value of $16,846,170 rather than at its aggregate cost of $17,931,679. In addition, as required by FAS No. 12, Clabir reported an unrealized loss on the USI stock of $1,085,509 in its income statement for the three-month period ending April 30, 1981. Invoking the lower of cost or market rule at the end of the second quarter of fiscal 1982, Clabir reported the USI stock at its aggregate cost of $17,931,679 since the market value of the stock exceeded its aggregate cost by several million dollars. In its second quarter income statement, Clabir recorded an unrealized gain of $1,085,509 which reversed the unrealized loss recorded the prior quarter on the USI stock.[1]

During the third quarter of fiscal 1982, the market value of Clabir's investment in USI stock fell more than $2 million below its aggregate cost. Nevertheless, in reporting the investment in its October 31, 1981, balance sheet Clabir used the aggregate cost figure of $23,494,623. Additionally, Clabir failed to report on its third quarter income statement an unrealized loss on the USI investment. Clabir management justified the decision not to write the USI stock down to its market value on October 31, 1981, by alleging that an oral offer had been received from USI executives to repurchase the stock at a price which exceeded the aggregate amount that Clabir had paid for it.[2] Footnote 5 of Clabir's October 31, 1981, financial statements disclosed this situation in the following manner.

> Marketable securities which consist principally of common stock of U.S. Industries, Inc. are stated at cost. The Company holds a 9.95% ownership of the common shares of U.S. Industries, Inc. Subsequent to the third

---

1. Because of the conservatism principle of accounting, FAS No. 12 allows companies to recognize unrealized gains on marketable securities only to the extent that unrealized losses have been recognized on those securities in prior reporting periods. Consequently, Clabir was allowed to record only a portion of the more than $5 million increase in the value of the USI stock during the second quarter of fiscal 1982.

2. A subsequent investigation by the SEC raised doubt as to whether the USI executives had made a valid offer to repurchase the USI stock held by Clabir.

quarter of fiscal 1982, the Company had engaged in discussions with representatives of U.S. Industries, Inc. and
others with respect to the possible sale by the Company
of its equity position in U.S. Industries, Inc. at a price in
excess of the Company's total cost of its investment. No
agreements have been reached during such discussions.[3]

By the end of the fourth quarter of fiscal 1982, the
USI executives, according to Clabir management, had
rescinded their offer to repurchase the USI stock held
by Clabir. Consequently, Clabir's year-end balance
sheet reported the investment in the USI stock at its
aggregate market value of $21,131,375, while the com-
pany's 1982 income statement reported an unrealized
loss on the stock of approximately $3.4 million.

After reviewing Clabir's quarterly financial statements for fiscal 1982, the SEC objected to the accounting treatment the company had applied to its investment in USI stock during the third quarter of that
year. In particular, the SEC maintained that the USI
investment should have been reported at its aggregate market value in Clabir's October 31, 1981, balance sheet and that an unrealized loss equal to the
difference between the aggregate market value and
aggregate cost of the investment should have been
included in the company's third quarter income statement. In justifying this position, the SEC argued
that the true market value of the USI stock as of
October 31, 1981, was the stock's closing price on
that date on the New York Stock Exchange (NYSE),
rather than the higher per share price at which USI

---

3. *Accounting and Auditing Enforcement Release No. 4*, Securities and
Exchange Commission (Washington, D.C.: U.S. Government Printing Office, 1983).

executives had allegedly offered to repurchase the stock. The SEC charged that Clabir, by failing to apply properly the lower of cost or market rule during the third quarter of fiscal 1982, had overstated its net income for that period by more than 58 percent and had overstated its total assets as well.[4] Clabir was eventually required by the SEC to amend its balance sheet and income statement for the third quarter of fiscal 1982.

The enforcement action taken by the SEC against Clabir Corporation sent a strong signal that the federal agency expected full compliance with the requirements of FAS No. 12. Prior to the issuance of that standard, the great majority of public companies had accounted for investments in marketable securities at historical cost. Apparently, many public companies were reluctant to implement FAS No. 12's lower of cost or market rule since doing so would effectively force them to reduce the reported value of an asset that was quite often a very significant item on their balance sheets. This reluctance allegedly resulted in certain companies, such as Clabir Corporation, employing subtle and not so subtle "gimmicks" to sidestep the requirements of FAS No. 12.

---

4. The SEC admitted that Clabir had disclosed in the footnotes to its quarterly financial statements why the USI stock was presented at its aggregate cost. However, the SEC ruled that the footnote describing this decision was inadequate since it did not identify the price per share at which USI executives had allegedly offered to repurchase the stock. In addition, the footnote failed to disclose that in prior quarters the closing price of the USI stock on the NYSE had been used as the market price in applying the lower of cost or market rule.

The adoption of FAS No. 12 in 1976 was probably most significant because it was one of the first measures taken by the accounting profession to quell mounting criticism of historical cost-based financial statements. Generally accepted accounting principles (GAAP) require, in most cases, that reporting entities list their assets in their periodic balance sheets at historical cost rather than some version of current value, such as market value, net realizable value, or replacement cost. Critics of the accounting profession have long contended that historical costs quickly lose their relevance to financial statement users. For instance, a factory that cost $20 million to build in 1965 may currently have a market value or replacement cost of several times that figure. For balance sheet purposes, however, the factory must be reported at its historical cost less accumulated depreciation.

The use of historical costs by accountants for financial reporting purposes was first widely criticized in the 1960s and 1970s when double-digit inflation rates resulted in large disparities between the cost and current value of many, if not most, assets of United States businesses. In the late 1970s, following the adoption of FAS No. 12, the SEC and the FASB responded to charges that high inflation was threatening the credibility and usefulness of historical cost-based financial data by requiring many companies to provide supplemental disclosures in their financial statements regarding the replacement cost of their assets. However, after inflation rates retreated during the early 1980s both the SEC and the FASB rescinded these supplemental disclosure requirements.

The next impetus for requiring companies to disclose current value data came in the late 1980s with the near total collapse of the savings and loan industry. Numerous parties alleged that a major contributing factor to the savings and loan debacle was the ability of financial institutions to report their assets, a large portion of which was typically commercial loans, at their historical cost. For a period of several years, literally hundreds of savings and loans that would have been insolvent had their asset portfolios been written down to market value continued to operate and extend loans on increasingly risky investment ventures. The SEC maintained that had savings and loans been required to use current value accounting in 1978, the industry, which appeared financially strong at the time, would have had a negative net worth well in excess of $100 billion.[5]

In 1989, with the appointment of Richard Breeden as the chairman of the SEC, the federal agency began an aggressive campaign to require public companies to disclose current value information in their financial statements. Following his appointment, Commissioner Breeden immediately began criticizing the use of historical costs in balance sheets. Breeden caustically suggested that if historical costs were to be reported in public companies' balance sheets, the headings of those financial statements should begin with the phrase "Once upon a time . . . "[6] Breeden and his top assistants repeatedly used the savings and loan industry as an example of how historical cost finan-

---

5. K.G. Salwen and R.G. Blumenthal, "Tackling Accounting, SEC Pushes Changes With Broad Impact," *Wall Street Journal* (September 27, 1990): A1, A12.

6. Ibid., A1.

cial statements can damage the credibility of the financial reporting process.

> Nothing does more to destroy the credibility of the financial reporting process, or the confidence of the investing public, than financial statements that create the impression all is well when in fact all is not well . . . You only have to look at the thrift [savings and loan] industry disaster to know what can happen when you travel too far down a path that ignores economic reality.[7]

The principal opponents of current value accounting are corporate executives, particularly those in industries, such as banking, that would be very adversely affected by a move away from historical costs. These individuals maintain that the use of current values are not feasible for financial reporting purposes for several reasons. The most obvious problem in implementing current value accounting is that market values or other readily determinable "current" values do not exist for many assets. Most marketable securities, of course, have a readily determinable market value at any point in time; however, to use an extreme example, what "market" value would corporate giants such as CBS, Apple Computer, and Coca–Cola attach to their world-famous logos—assets which are obviously extremely valuable but carried at only nominal amounts in these entities' accounting records? A related problem is that the lack of objective current values would invite many companies to overstate intentionally the reported values of their assets, a problem experienced in Australia, a country which allows

---

7. *Journal of Accountancy,* "SEC Market Value Conference: Experts Urge Mark–to–Market," vol. 173 (January 1992): 13–16.

companies to report noncurrent assets at their market value.

The cost of obtaining current value data and the fact that current values cannot be used for taxation purposes are additional limitations of current value accounting. Finally, critics of current value accounting point out that the volatility of corporate earnings would increase greatly if current values, rather than historical costs, were used for financial reporting purposes. The experience of companies such as Clabir Corporation that have had a large portion of their assets accounted for at the lower of cost or market for many years because of FAS No. 12 illustrates this point very clearly. An increase in the volatility of corporate earnings has economic consequences for reporting entities as well as investors and creditors since it significantly increases the financial risk associated with lending and investing activities.

In spite of these implementation problems, proponents of current value accounting continue to maintain that the use of some form of current values for financial reporting purposes is the only way to restore the credibility of external financial statements. Probably one of the strongest arguments for adopting current values for external reporting purposes is the fact that companies make extensive use of them for internal decision making purposes, a point made repeatedly by representatives of the SEC. In this vein, one corporate executive noted that his company utilizes current values for internal purposes to assess "real performance."

> We may not be accurate in our current cost estimates, but we're a hell of a lot closer than erroneous historical-cost

basis . . . [Current value accounting] helps you focus on what your real performance is.[8]

Clearly, if internal decision makers use current values to make economic decisions, it seems reasonable to assume that investors, creditors, and other external decision makers would find such data useful as well.

QUESTIONS

1. Clabir management failed to properly apply the lower of cost or market rule to its investment in USI stock at the end of the third quarter of fiscal 1982. However, this rule was correctly applied at the end of the fourth quarter of 1982, resulting in a proper accounting for the investment in USI stock in Clabir's 1982 financial statements. Given that the investment in the USI stock was properly reported in Clabir's 1982 balance sheet and that the unrealized loss on that stock was included in the company's 1982 income statement, why did the SEC sanction the company for the improper accounting decision made during the third quarter of that year?

2. Short-term investments, such as Clabir Corporation's investment in USI stock, are accounted for on a lower of cost or market basis. Give other examples of assets for which present accounting standards require or permit a departure from historical cost-basis accounting. Why are these departures required or permitted?

---

8. "Tackling Accounting, SEC Pushes Changes With Broad Impact," A12.

3. Briefly discuss what are, in your opinion, the best methods to use in arriving at current values for the following assets: buildings, patents, furniture and fixtures, finished goods inventory, and work-in-process inventory.

4. Critics of current value accounting contend that it could be used to manipulate the reported profits of companies. Give examples of how companies can manipulate their reported profits using historical cost-based accounting.

5. Most of the attention in the debate over historical cost vs. current value accounting has focused on the asset side of the balance sheet. Could current value accounting be applied to the liability side of the balance sheet? If so, briefly discuss how this would be accomplished.

6. Assume that Jenco, Inc., has the following balance sheet on January 1, 1995.

Cash	$4,000,000
Land	5,000,000
Preferred stock	3,000,000
Common stock	4,000,000
Retained earnings	2,000,000

The company will pay $90,000 in dividends annually to the preferred stockholders for the period 1995–1997 and must redeem the preferred stock on December 31, 1997. Assume that the land owned by the company was purchased on January 1, 1995, for $5,000,000. Also assume that from January 1, 1995, through December 31, 1997, the land increases in value by $1,500,000 and that the consumer price index

(CPI) increases from 100 to 120. Ignoring tax considerations, how much "better off" are the common stockholders of Jenco on December 31, 1997, versus January 1, 1995? Explain. Assuming the company redeems the preferred stock on December 31, 1997, but retains the land, prepare a new balance sheet for the company at the end of 1997. Does this balance sheet reflect "economic reality"? Why or why not?

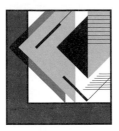

Case 4.3
Insiders, Iniquity,
and Internal Control

Employee theft is a problem that cuts across organizations of all sizes and types. Probably most susceptible to this problem, however, are retail companies that sell relatively inexpensive items and process a large number of cash transactions each day. A recent study of supermarkets, for instance, estimated that the average total cash and merchandise loss per employee in those business establishments is more than $20 per week; a similar study found that automotive supply retailers may lose as much as 10 percent of their inventory to employee theft.[1] Surprisingly, the

1. S. Feinstein, "Worker Theft Imposes Rising Cost on Retailers and Customers," *Wall Street Journal* (February 20, 1990): A1; P. Sebastian, "Internal Theft of Car Parts Deepens Inventory Losses at Auto Dealerships," *Wall Street Journal* (October 17, 1991): A1.

worst offenders are often employees whom employers least suspect of being dishonest. In one recent case, a saleswoman who had been named employee of the year three consecutive years by her Florida-based company confessed to an investigative agency that she had stolen hundreds of thousands of dollars of merchandise over a period of several years.[2] Likewise, a company lost thousands of dollars of merchandise due to thefts by a well-liked and energetic warehouse supervisor who insisted on staying late each night to help "clean up" after all of his subordinates had gone home.[3]

On a cumulative basis, losses due to employee theft are staggering in magnitude. Although arriving at a precise estimate of these losses is impossible, by the early 1990s experts predicted that employee theft was costing United States businesses at least $40 billion annually and that fully one-third of all business failures were attributable to this problem.[4]

Recent history has proven that white collar executives can also do tremendous damage to their employers and to the stockholders of their companies. Among the classic management fraud cases in recent history is the Equity Funding scandal of the early 1970s. At the time, Equity Funding was one of the largest life insurance companies in the nation, and, according to industry statistics, the fastest growing.

2. S. Shellenbarger, "Holidays Are Time for Firms To Be Vigilant," *Wall Street Journal* (December 24, 1990): 9, 10.

3. Ibid.

4. M. Hanif, "Making Honesty an Employee's Best Policy," *Washington Post* (October 7, 1991): WB 10.

Unfortunately for investors in the New York Stock Exchange company more than one-half of its reported revenues were non-existent. To reach target revenue and profit goals established for the company, its top executives, with the assistance of dozens of their subordinates, created tens of thousands of bogus life insurance policies that had allegedly been sold by the company sales staff. The Equity Funding scam was eventually exposed by an embittered former employee who revealed the fraudulent scheme to the press. More recently, the ESM Government Securities and ZZZZ Best Company management fraud scandals of the 1980s each inflicted more than $100 million of losses on stockholders and creditors.

PREVENTING INSIDER FRAUD AND THEFT: THE ROLE OF THE INTERNAL CONTROL STRUCTURE

The principal means that an organization uses to prevent and detect insider fraud is its internal control structure. The technical literature of the accounting profession defines an internal control structure as the "policies and procedures established to provide reasonable assurance that specific entity objectives will be achieved." [5] Safeguarding an organization's assets and ensuring that an organization can generate relia-

---

5. *Statement on Auditing Standards No. 55, Consideration of the Internal Control Structure in a Financial Statement Audit* (New York: American Institute of Certified Public Accountants, 1988).

ble periodic financial statements are two of these objectives.

Internal control structures are composed of three elements: a control environment, an accounting system, and a set of control procedures. A company's accounting system consists of the methods and records it uses to record transactions. A given company's general ledger, purchases journal, and accounts receivable subsidiary ledger, for example, would be considered components of its accounting system. Control procedures, on the other hand, are the specific policies or rules that an entity establishes to accomplish its primary organizational objectives. One of the most important types of control procedures is the segregation of key functional responsibilities within an organization. For instance, employees should not have custodial and recordkeeping responsibility for cash since they could steal a portion of the cash and conceal the theft by making the appropriate entries in the accounting records.

The most important element of an organization's internal control structure is the control environment, which essentially represents the degree of "control consciousness" within the organization. Executives are ultimately responsible for making employees aware of the critical role that administrative and accounting controls play in ensuring that an organization operates efficiently and effectively. If the actions of top executives suggest that maintaining a strong internal control structure is not one of their top priorities, then their subordinates will likely exhibit little control consciousness as well.

E.F. Hutton & Co., the second largest brokerage firm in the nation until the mid–1980s, provides an excellent example of what can happen to an organization that has an inadequate control environment. Another high-profile organization that experienced problems with its internal control structure during the 1980s was the Los Angeles Dodgers professional baseball club. Unlike E.F. Hutton & Co., the Dodger organization was, and is, characterized by a strong control environment in which top executives lead by example. However, the Dodger case illustrates that even in an organization that places considerable importance on control consciousness, breakdowns in its financial controls can occur leaving the organization vulnerable to opportunistic employees.

CASHING IN ON WEAK INTERNAL CONTROLS: THE CASE OF E.F. HUTTON & CO.

Edward F. Hutton was born into a poor family in 1876 in New York City. Fatherless by the age of ten, Hutton dropped out of school as a teenager to help support his family. After working short stints at one menial job after another, Hutton became intrigued by the securities industry, particularly the financial opportunities it offered. Hutton had worked as a stockbroker for several years with little success when he met and married the daughter of a prominent and wealthy New York City broker. With the help of his father-in-law, Hutton established a small brokerage firm of his own. A few months later, the ambitious and opportunistic Hutton recognized the market potential for the securities industry on the rapidly growing West Coast and opened an office of his firm in San Francisco.

Ironically, the devastating San Francisco earthquake of 1906 was largely responsible for the eventual financial success of E.F. Hutton & Co. Hutton's direct telegraph line to New York City was one of the few, possibly the only, means of communication to the East Coast immediately following the 1906 quake. Since no other brokerage on Wall Street was aware of the earthquake for several hours, the Hutton firm was able to use that short period of time to pile up significant trading profits for itself and its customers. Such ingenuity was cultivated and rewarded at E.F. Hutton & Co. over its entire existence. Top management was disdainful of bureaucratic policies, centralized decision-making, and organizational charts, all of which Edward F. Hutton believed stifled employee creativity. Instead, employees were strongly encouraged to exercise their own judgment and to be innovative, particularly when it came to enhancing the profitability of the brokerage firm.

The Hutton firm's free-wheeling corporate culture was manifested in a number of ways in its business practices, one of the more notorious being the cash management methods used by the company. These practices first became the subject of public scrutiny in the early 1980s when Bank of America, a large West Coast bank, discovered that its electronic processing equipment was rejecting a disproportionately large percentage of Hutton's checks.

Historically, Bank of America had experienced a one percent rejection rate for checks processed by its electronic equipment, but the rejection rate for Hutton's checks by the early 1980s was approaching 50 percent.

The rejection of a check by a bank's electronic scanning equipment forces bank personnel to process the check manually, thus adding, often significantly, to the amount of time required for the check to clear the bank on which it was written. Methods used to cause a check to be rejected for automatic processing include tampering with the micro-encoding line (such as stapling the check at that point), bending the corners, and smearing a small quantity of a foreign substance on the check's surface (vaseline is apparently the foreign substance of choice among check tamperers). When the check-clearing problem at Bank of America was brought to the attention of Hutton, it was quickly resolved to the satisfaction of Bank of America's executives and no criminal or civil actions were brought against the brokerage firm as a result.

Subsequent to the check-clearing problem that Bank of America experienced with Hutton, the United States Justice Department announced that it was investigating the large brokerage firm's cash management practices. The focus of this investigation was Hutton's so called drawdown system. This system allowed Hutton to minimize its cash balances in noninterest-bearing collection accounts maintained in communities where its retail sales offices were located. Through a complex equation, each retail office of Hutton would estimate by 1:00 P.M. of each business day the dollar value of customer remittances that would be available by the end of that day in its local collection account. That amount of funds would then be transferred by wire from the collection account to an interest-bearing regional clearing account.

Gradually, over several years, many of Hutton's branch managers began abusing the drawdown system. Since the managers were paid 10 percent of the interest profits of their branch as a year-end bonus, they had an incentive to drawdown excessive amounts in their local collection accounts. For instance, in one case, Hutton's drawdown equation indicated that $70,000 would be available for withdrawal at the end of a certain branch's business day. Instead of transferring that amount, however, the branch manager transferred approximately 100 times that amount, or $7,000,000, to his regional clearing account. Of course, such excessive withdrawals resulted in Hutton's local collection acccounts being overdrawn, overdrafts that occasionally exceeded the entire capital of the affected banks.[6]

The cash overdrafts caused by branch managers abusing the drawdown system were, in most cases, quite modest. Nevertheless, when accumulated for all of Hutton's branches, the total of these overdrafts had reached a staggering one-half billion dollars by the end of 1983. The collective impact of Hutton's cash management practices on its income statement was also dramatic. In 1981, interest profits accounted for

---

6. Why would banks allow Hutton branch managers to continually overdraft their local collection accounts was a question regulatory authorities posed during their investigation of the brokerage firm. First, Hutton apparently used the overdrafting scheme on a recurring basis only with its smaller banks, principally the banks that serviced Hutton's small to moderately sized retail offices. These banks were apparently either too naive to realize that they were being defrauded or accepted the overdrafts as an implicit cost of doing business with the prestigious brokerage firm. Second, although there were numerous cases of enormous overdrafts, most Hutton branch managers involved in the overdrafting scheme were much more conservative.

almost three-fourths of the net income of the firm's retail brokerage division, an abnormally high percentage for the brokerage industry.

In the spring of 1985, following a lengthy investigation by the United States Justice Department, E.F. Hutton & Co. pled guilty to 2,000 counts of mail and wire fraud, charges stemming from the use of the nation's postal service and telecommunications networks by Hutton to defraud its banks via the drawdown system. The fallout from this scandal eventually drove the firm to the brink of insolvency before it was bought out in 1988 by Shearson Lehman Brothers, one of its major competitors.

Surprisingly, the United States Justice Department was never able to pinpoint exactly who in the organization was responsible for authorizing or permitting the abusive cash management practices. Hutton's top executives steadfastly maintained that they had never encouraged branch managers to abuse the drawdown system. Conversely, the branch managers contended that they were encouraged to be very aggressive in using the system. The lack of adequate documentation regarding the firm's internal procedures eventually forced the Justice Department to bring charges against the firm as a whole rather than filing charges against individuals within the firm. In a subsequent congressional investigation of the Hutton scandal, one United States representative maintained that the firm's top executives had purposefully created a corporate culture that encouraged their subordinates to engage in illicit, profit-maximizing activities. At the same time, these executives, according to the congressman, had intentionally established an extremely weak internal control structure so that it would be impossible for them to be held accountable for the irresponsible and/or illegal actions of their subordinates.

> We have fixed our posteriors to these chairs, now, for weeks in a row, and the only thing we're getting out of witnesses is "Well, don't look at me, look at the other guy. You know, I didn't know, I didn't ask a question, I didn't hear it, I wasn't there when it happened." Everything is built on plausible deniability—construct the situation, the scenario, so everybody can deny they were a part of it, and yet the thing goes on merrily down the road. And nobody but nobody is ever involved.[7]

DODGER BLUE: PADDING THE PAYROLL

In 1890, the Brooklyn Trolley Dodgers professional baseball team joined the National League. Over the years, the Dodgers would have considerable difficulty competing with the other baseball teams in the New York City area, teams which generally were much better financed and, as a result, stocked with higher caliber players. In 1958, after nearly seven decades of mostly frustration on and off the baseball field, the Dodgers shocked the sports world by moving to Los Angeles. Walter O'Malley, the flamboyant owner of the Dodgers at the time, saw an opportunity to introduce professional baseball to the rapidly growing population of southern California and, more importantly, an opportunity to make his team more profitable. As an inducement to the Dodgers, Los Angeles County

---

7. Committee on the Judiciary, House of Representatives, *E.F. Hutton Mail and Wire Fraud Case, Part 2* (Washington, D.C.: U.S. Government Printing Office, 1986).

purchased a goat farm located in Chavez Ravine, an area two miles northwest of downtown Los Angeles, and gave the property to O'Malley for the site of his new baseball stadium.

Since moving to Los Angeles, the Dodgers have been the envy of the baseball world. "In everything from profit to stadium maintenance . . . the Dodgers are the prototype of how a franchise should be run." [8] During the decade of the 1980s, the Dodgers were reportedly the most profitable franchise in baseball with a pre-tax profit margin approaching 25 percent in many years. By 1990, the franchise, still owned by the O'Malley family, was valued at an incredible $250,000,000. Peter O'Malley, the current president of the Dodgers, attributes the success of his organization to the experts he has retained in all functional areas. "I don't have to be an expert on taxes, split-fingered fastballs, or labor relations with our ushers. That talent is all available." [9]

Edward Campos, a long-time accountant for the Dodgers, was seemingly a perfect example of the experts in the Dodgers organization to whom Peter O'Malley alluded. Campos accepted a position with the Dodgers as a young man and by 1986, after almost two decades with the club, had worked his way up the employment hierarchy to become the operations payroll chief, a job with considerable prestige in the organization. After taking charge of the payroll department, Campos designed and implemented a

8. R.J. Harris, "Forkball for Dodgers: Costs Up, Gate Off," *Wall Street Journal* (August 31, 1990): B1, B4.

9. Ibid., B1.

new payroll system, a system that reportedly only he fully understood. In fact, Campos controlled the system so completely that he personally filled out the weekly payroll cards for each of the Dodgers' 400 employees. Campos was known not only for his work ethic but also for his loyalty to the club and its owners. " . . . the Dodgers trusted him, and when he was on vacation, he even came back and did the payroll." [10]

Unfortunately, the Dodgers' trust in Campos was misplaced. Over a period of several years, Campos embezzled several hundred thousand dollars from the Dodgers organization. According to court records, Campos padded the Dodgers' payroll by adding a number of fictitious employees to various departments in the organization. In addition, Campos inflated the number of hours worked by several employees and then split the resulting overpayments 50–50 with those individuals. The fraudulent scheme was finally discovered when Campos was unable to work for a period of time due to illness and his responsibilities were assumed temporarily by the Dodgers' controller. While completing the payroll one week, the controller happened to notice that several employees, including ushers, security guards and ticket salespeople, were being paid unusually large amounts. In some cases, employees earning $7 per hour were receiving weekly paychecks approaching $2,000. Following a criminal investigation and the filing of charges against Campos and his cohorts, all of

10. P. Feldman, "7 Accused of Embezzling $332,583 From Dodgers," *Los Angeles Times* (September 17, 1986): Section II, 1, 6.

the individuals in the payroll fraud confessed. After pleading guilty to embezzlement charges, Campos was sentenced to eight years in state prison and agreed to make restitution of approximately $132,000 to the Dodgers. Another of the conspirators also received a prison sentence, while the remaining individuals involved in the scam made restitution and were placed on probation.

QUESTIONS

1. Many of the recent highly publicized cases of management fraud and employee theft have involved individuals who had a history of perpetrating such crimes. What internal controls can organizations establish to minimize the likelihood that they will hire employees who have engaged in unethical or illegal behavior in the past?

2. Most retail companies maintain accounts receivable and accounts payable subsidiary ledgers. What are the principal control objectives associated with the maintenance of these accounting records? What are the control objectives related to the preparation of a monthly bank reconciliation for an entity's bank accounts?

3. In your opinion, which party or parties within E.F. Hutton & Company should have been held responsible for the illegal cash management practices being used by the firm? Explain.

4. Regarding the Dodgers case, what were the major control weaknesses in that organization's payroll transaction cycle? What control procedures might have resulted in the prevention or detection of the fraudulent scheme?

5. Many organizations have established internal audit departments to strengthen their internal control structures. Define, in general terms, the responsibilities typically assigned to internal auditors. Discuss how internal auditors might have been put to effective use in both the Hutton and Los Angeles Dodgers cases.

6. Visit three local retail establishments and observe the operations of each entity for a period of time. For each establishment, record five internal control procedures that you observed and one internal control weakness which was evident. Write a short report summarizing your findings. Include in your report the purpose of each of the internal controls you identified and recommendations regarding how each of the internal control weaknesses you observed could be eliminated or its impact on the establishment minimized.

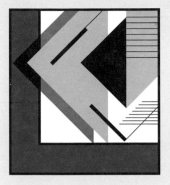

Section Five

Ethics and the Accountant

Case 5.1
Irving Goldberg,
Corporate Accountant

Irving Goldberg joined the accounting department of Republic Carloading & Distributing Company during World War II. Nearly two decades later, Goldberg's hard work and dedication to his employer were rewarded when he was promoted to treasurer of the company. Republic's principal line of business was freight forwarding which involves consolidating partial railroad carloads of freight shipments into full carloads and then forwarding the individual items of freight to their ultimate destinations. In May 1963, Goldberg became an employee of Yale Express System, Inc., when that company acquired Republic. Yale Express, a publicly owned firm, was much smaller than Republic and engaged principally in short-haul trucking at the time. Yale Express was founded in 1938 by Benjamin Eskow, and twenty-five years later the company was still effectively controlled by the Eskow family, which held 61 percent of its outstanding common stock.

Following the takeover of Republic by Yale Express, Goldberg remained the treasurer of Republic, which was operated as a wholly owned subsidiary of its parent company. In his capacity as treasurer, Goldberg was responsible for monitoring and controlling the cash disbursements and receipts of Republic. At the same time, Goldberg also served as Republic's principal accounting executive. As such, Goldberg was responsible for making the major accounting decisions for the company and for supervising the preparation of Republic's periodic internal and external financial statements. The accounting decisions made by Goldberg had a significant impact on the reported operating results and financial condition of Yale Express since the latter's consolidated financial statements included the financial data of Republic.

Within a matter of months after the acquisition of Republic, executives of Yale Express began pressuring Goldberg to manipulate Republic's reported operating results. Apparently, most of this pressure was applied by Fred Mackensen, the administrative vice-president of Yale Express and an individual who had been instrumental in arranging the takeover of Republic. In subsequent lawsuits filed against Yale Express and its officers in the late 1960s, Goldberg testified that Mackensen wanted to report a profit of $250,000 for Republic during September 1963 even though Goldberg's figures showed that the company had posted a small loss during that period. A few months later, in January 1964, Mackensen was upset by a $900,000 loss reported for Republic by Goldberg. Allegedly, Mackensen would not accept Republic's operating results for that month until the loss had been reduced to approximately $100,000.

According to Goldberg's courtroom testimony, he and Mackensen had serious disagreements regarding the accounting methods that Goldberg was employing for Republic. The most heated disagreement apparently concerned Goldberg's method of estimating Republic's unrecorded transportation expenses at the end of each fiscal year. Because the railroads and trucking companies that Republic dealt with were slow in submitting invoices for their services, Goldberg and his subordinates were forced to estimate the amount of such expenses that should be recorded as an accrued liability at the end of each fiscal year. Historically, Republic had incurred approximately $.84 of transportation charges for each $1 of earned revenue. However, Mackensen decided that the accrual rate should be only $.78 per $1 of revenue for the fiscal year ending December 31, 1963.

According to Goldberg's analysis, the change implemented by Mackensen in the accrual percentage for year-end transportation expenses resulted in an overstatement of Republic's Net Income for 1963 of approximately $1 million. Even though Goldberg was aware that Republic's financial statements were materially in error, he signed a report filed by the company with the Interstate Commerce Commission which indicated that the statements were accurate. The following year, the 1963 consolidated financial statements of Yale Express, which included the erroneous financial statements of Republic, were used by company executives to obtain a multimillion dollar loan from a syndicate of insurance companies. When asked to explain why he vouched for the accuracy of the misrepresented financial statements of Republic, Goldberg replied that at the time he approved the statements he was not acting responsibly because he was under extreme duress.

During the course of the subsequent litigation in which Yale Express and its top executives became involved, Goldberg was questioned regarding whether or not Yale Express's accounting firm, Peat Marwick, was aware that the company's 1963 consolidated financial statements were materially in error. According to Goldberg's testimony, Peat Marwick challenged the sufficiency of Republic's year-end accrual of transportation expenses. Peat Marwick maintained that the transportation expense accrual was understated by nearly $2 million. Goldberg reported that after the accrual was increased by $975,000, Peat Marwick accepted the adjusted account balance as being materially accurate even though it was still significantly understated. During cross-examination, Goldberg was asked if he had informed Peat Marwick that the 1963 Yale Express financial statements about to be reported on by the accounting firm were materially misstated, even after the posting of the large adjustment. Goldberg replied, "I did not. I couldn't have cared less." [1]

---

1. *Wall Street Journal*, "Former Official of Unit of Yale Express Claims Mental Irresponsibility" (October 14, 1968): 8.

In April 1964, Goldberg voluntarily took a leave of absence from Republic. Since January of that year, he had been under psychiatric care and had been taking sedatives to help him cope with the stress being imposed on him by his superiors. When he returned to Republic in May 1964, Goldberg was informed that he had been demoted to a clerk's position, chief of disbursements. Shortly thereafter, he discovered that two large adjusting entries had been posted to Republic's accounting records during his absence. These entries, which had been initialed by Mackensen, reduced Republic's transportation expenses for the first quarter of 1964 by $600,000. At this point, Goldberg went to the board of directors of Yale Express and reported that Republic's operating results were being grossly misrepresented. As a result of Goldberg's allegation, Peat Marwick was retained by the company's board of directors to perform an independent analysis of Republic's transportation expenses. The results of the Peat Marwick investigation supported Goldberg's claim. In fact, subsequent courtroom testimony would demonstrate that Yale Express incurred a loss of nearly $1.8 million in 1963 even though the company initially reported a profit of almost $2 million for that year. A significant portion of the misrepresentation of the company's operating results for 1963 was attributable to the understatement of the year-end accrual for Republic's transportation expenses.

Following the completion of the Peat Marwick investigation of Republic's transportation expenses, Goldberg requested that he be allowed to report directly to Eskow rather than to Mackensen. Apparently, Goldberg was increasingly uncomfortable with the pressure being exerted on him by Mackensen to improve the reported operating results of Republic. Goldberg also reportedly warned Eskow that Yale Express's financial condition was deteriorating very rapidly, primarily as a result of Republic's poor operating results, and that the company could possibly face bankruptcy in the near future. Eskow ignored Goldberg's request that he not be required to report to Mackensen. Eskow also disagreed with Goldberg's assessment of the company's financial condition and eventually asked the long-time employee to resign. Goldberg refused to leave Republic, stating that his personal financial situation would not allow him to do so. A short time later, however, Goldberg was fired by Mackensen, who justified the dismissal by stating that Goldberg's position was no longer needed by the company.

In 1965, following the disclosure of the fraudulent financial statements released by Yale Express in 1963 and 1964, both Eskow and Mackensen were forced to resign their positions with the company. Shortly thereafter, Yale Express filed for protection from its creditors under the federal bankruptcy laws. In November 1968, Eskow and Mackensen were convicted on more than thirty counts of fraud as a result of the misrepresented financial statements issued by Yale Express during 1963 and 1964. The principal prosecution witness in that trial was Irving Goldberg. In addition to the criminal lawsuits filed against Eskow and Mackensen, several large class action lawsuits were filed against Yale Express, its officers, and its accounting firm, Peat Marwick. Those lawsuits were eventually settled out of court for undisclosed sums.

QUESTIONS

1. Why is it necessary for a company to record a liability at year-end for its unpaid expenses? Explain how understating the accrual of a company's unpaid expenses at year-end affects its reported operating results and financial condition.

2. Identify the alternative courses of action that were available to Irving Goldberg in late 1963 when he was being pressured by Mackensen to manipulate Republic's reported operating results. Which of these alternatives would have been most appropriate for him to choose under the circumstances?

3. What party or parties are primarily responsible for ensuring that a company's financial statements are materially accurate? In the case of Yale Express, identify this party or parties.

4. Identify the principal parties who were affected by the issuance of the materially misrepresented financial statements of Yale Express. How were these parties affected?

5. Goldberg testified in court that he did not inform Peat Marwick, Yale Express's auditors, that the 1963 financial statements of Yale Express were materially misstated even after the year-end transportation accrual was increased by $975,000. Quite often, the relationship between independent auditors and client personnel is perceived to be adversarial in nature. Research the issue of auditor-client relationships and then write an essay discussing how poor relationships between auditors and their client personnel can affect the quality of independent audits. Also identify in your essay measures that accounting firms can take to minimize this problem. (Note: The **Accountants' Index**, an annual compendium of accounting-related articles which is published by the American Institute of Certified Public Accountants, would be a very helpful source of references for your essay.)

CASE 5.2
ETHICAL DILEMMAS
AND THE INDEPENDENT
AUDITOR: LESSONS LEARNED
FROM THE 1980S[1]

The decade of the 1980s was a very difficult period for financial institutions of all types, including banks, savings and loans, and brokerage firms. Literally hundreds of billions of dollars in losses were suffered by the savings and loan industry alone. When the insurance fund of the Federal Savings and Loan Insurance Corporation (FSLIC) was depleted in the mid–1980s,

1. I would like to acknowledge the assistance of Carol Tankersley in developing this case.

the United States Congress was forced to pass legislation to approve a huge bailout plan to prevent the savings and loan industry from totally collapsing. As the losses of financial institutions reached staggering amounts, taxpayers demanded that the parties responsible for those losses be held accountable. One of the parties singled out to shoulder a seemingly disproportionate share of this responsibility was the public accounting profession, particularly the large national and international public accounting firms that had audited many of the financial institutions that failed during the 1980s.

Public accounting firms provide four distinct types of services to their clients: taxation services, bookkeeping, management consulting services, and independent audits. Auditing is the primary source of revenue for the largest public accounting firms which employ thousands of CPAs and have offices in most major U.S. cities. These large accounting firms, often referred to as audit firms, are retained to examine, or "audit," the financial statements of their clients. The principal purpose of such an audit is to determine whether an entity's financial statements fairly present its financial condition at a specific point in time and its results of operations and cash flows for a given period of time.

Audits are necessary because business executives have an incentive to "window dress" their firms' financial statements for a number of reasons. For instance, the top officials of a company may embellish its financial statements to influence a local banker's decision regarding a loan application made by the firm. By obtaining an independent, expert opinion on the fairness of their firms' financial statements, business executives enhance the credibility of those statements and increase the likelihood that third parties will rely on the statements in making investment and lending decisions. If companies did not obtain independent audits of their financial statements, theoretically, each individual using those statements would be forced to analyze the records from which they were drawn to determine whether the statements were reliable. The federal securities laws require that all publicly owned companies have their annual financial statements audited; however, many privately owned companies obtain audits voluntarily for the benefit of their banks, creditors, and other interested parties.

Since its inception, the distinguishing trait of the audit function in the United States has been the required independence of auditors from their clients. If auditors are not independent or not perceived to be independent of their clients, the opinions they issue on their clients' financial statements will be of little use to third parties. As savings and loans, banks, and other financial institutions began failing during the 1980s, critics of the accounting profession began questioning the independence of auditors. These critics suggested that, in many cases, auditors were aware of the poor financial health of their financial institution clients or of the fraudulent schemes they were using to misrepresent their financial affairs. However, because these auditors were allegedly not independent of their clients, they chose to further compromise the ethical norms of their profession by not disclosing such information to the public.

The fact that auditors are hired and compensated by the companies they audit is the key aspect of the auditor-client relationship that threatens the independence of auditors. If an audit firm issues something other than an unqualified opinion on a client's financial statements, the client's executives may choose to "get even" the following year by selecting another firm to audit their company's financial statements. Critics suggest that this leverage that client executives have on their auditors may cause auditing firms, on occasion, "to look the other way" when they discover errors or other problems in their clients' financial statements.

The following vignettes describe three of the most publicized cases of the 1980s which called into question the independence of auditors of failed financial institutions. Studying ethical dilemmas confronted by auditors in the past should help audit professionals in the future to cope with such problematic situations as constructively as possible.

Act I

On August 1, 1979, Jose Gomez achieved his long-sought goal of becoming a partner with a major public accounting firm. On that date, Gomez was promoted to partner by Alexander Grant & Company, the tenth largest public accounting firm in the U.S. at the time. Only thirty-one years old, the outgoing and charming Gomez was recognized by his fellow partners as an individual who would almost certainly rise to the upper management ranks of Alexander Grant during his career. Shortly after his promotion, Gomez, whose specialty was auditing, was named the managing partner of the Fort Lauderdale office of Alexander Grant. Unfortunately, Gomez never realized his full potential. In March 1987, Gomez began serving a twelve-year term in a federal prison in Tallahassee, Florida, after pleading guilty to forgery and fraud charges.

Ironically, Gomez's fate was sealed just a few days following his promotion to partner. During a lunch with Alan Novick, an officer of his largest audit client, Gomez was startled by Novick's admission that the client's audited financial statements of the prior two years, 1977 and 1978, contained material errors. The client, ESM Government Securities, Inc., a Fort Lauderdale brokerage firm specializing in government securities, had several million dollars in losses in both 1977 and 1978 that Novick had successfully concealed from the Alexander Grant auditors, including Gomez.

Since the unqualified audit opinions issued on the ESM financial statements for those two years had been personally authorized by Gomez, Novick warned him that the disclosure of the material errors could jeopardize his career with Alexander Grant. According to Gomez, Novick repeatedly goaded him with comments such as, "It's going to look terrible for you . . . and you just got promoted to partner." [2] Novick attempted to convince Gomez that ESM could recoup the losses that had been hidden from Alexander Grant but only if Gomez agreed not to withdraw the unqualified audit opinions issued on the firm's 1977 and 1978 financial statements. If

2. M. Brannigan, "Auditor's Downfall Shows a Man Caught in Trap of His Own Making," *Wall Street Journal* (March 4, 1987): 33.

Gomez insisted on withdrawing the audit opinions, ESM would fail and a number of parties would suffer, including the customers of ESM and Gomez. Eventually, Gomez capitulated and agreed not to disclose the material errors in ESM's prior financial statements.

When Novick met with Gomez and admitted that ESM's 1977 and 1978 financial statements contained material errors, he was apparently aware that Gomez was experiencing considerable financial problems. Although Gomez was earning a sizable salary as a partner of a major public accounting firm, that salary was not sufficient to support the affluent lifestyle he had adopted. After Gomez agreed to remain silent regarding the ESM fraud, Novick offered to help relieve his financial problems. In November 1979, Novick issued a $20,000 check to Gomez to cover past due credit card bills. The following year, after Gomez reportedly complained to Novick that his financial condition had worsened, Novick provided him with an additional $60,000. Court records document that over the course of the seven-year ESM fraud, Gomez received approximately $200,000 from ESM officials.

If Gomez actually believed at the time, as he subsequently alleged, that ignoring the material errors in the ESM financial statements was the best decision for all parties concerned, he was wrong—very wrong. The relatively small unreported losses in the 1977 and 1978 financial statements of ESM would grow to collective unreported losses of more than $300 million by the spring of 1985. Unlike most financial scandals which typically affect the stockholders and creditors of only a few companies, the ESM scandal triggered a series of events that would eventually rock both the national and international financial markets.

ESM's largest customer, Home State Savings, was an Ohio bank that was owed approximately $145 million by ESM when the latter ceased operations in March 1985. Home State Savings happened to be the largest of more than seventy Ohio banks whose deposits were not insured by the Federal Deposit Insurance Corporation (FDIC) but rather by a private insurance fund which these banks had formed. When Home State collapsed following the closure of ESM, panic stricken investors triggered runs on the other privately insured Ohio banks. Within a matter of days, the governor of Ohio decided to close all of the state's privately insured banks while state and federal regulatory authorities worked around the clock to prevent ESM's economic fallout from spreading further.

The closure of the Ohio banks and a growing loss of consumer confidence in the government securities market destabilized all of the nation's capital markets. At the peak of the crisis, the value of the United States dollar plunged 14 percent in the international markets in one day as foreign investors feared the entire United States banking system was in jeopardy.

ACT II

In 1978, Charles Keating, Jr., founded American Continental Corporation (ACC) in Ohio. Six years later, ACC acquired Lincoln Savings and Loan Association, a California-based company. In his application to purchase Lincoln, Keating pledged to regulatory authorities that he would retain the Lincoln management team, not use large deposits from money brokers to expand the size of the savings and loan, and ensure that residential home loans remained Lincoln's principal line of business. Shortly after gaining control of Lincoln, Keating replaced the savings and loan's management team, began accepting large deposits from money brokers allowing him to nearly triple the size of Lincoln in two years, and shifted the focus of Lincoln's lending activity from residential properties to high-risk real estate development projects.

On April 14, 1989, the Federal Home Loan Bank Board seized control of Lincoln Savings and Loan alleging that it was dissipating its assets by operating in an unsafe and unsound manner. On that date, Lincoln's balance sheet reported total assets of $5.3 billion, only 2.3 percent of which were investments in residential mortgage loans. Nearly two-thirds of Lincoln's asset portfolio was invested directly or indirectly in real estate development projects. At the time, federal authorities estimated that the closure of Lincoln Savings and Loan would eventually cost American taxpayers $2 billion, a figure that proved to be significantly understated.

The congressional hearings into the collapse of Lincoln Savings and Loan focused national attention on the failure of Lincoln's independent auditors to expose fraudulent real estate transactions that allowed the savings and loan to report millions of dollars of nonexistent profits. Of primary concern to the congressional committee investigating the collapse of Lincoln Savings and Loan were the 1986 and 1987 audits of Lincoln performed by Arthur Young & Company. In each of those years, Arthur Young rendered an unqualified opinion on Lincoln's financial statements despite concerns being expressed by regulatory authorities regarding certain questionable business practices of the savings and loan.

Following the completion of the 1987 audit of Lincoln by Arthur Young, the engagement audit partner, Jack Atchison, resigned from Arthur Young and accepted a position with ACC. Subsequent testimony would disclose that Atchison was earning approximately $225,000 with Arthur Young prior to his resignation; the position that Atchison accepted with ACC came with a salary of $930,000. The congressional investigative committee was alarmed by the close relationship that Atchison had developed with Keating prior to resigning from Arthur Young. Testimony before the committee disclosed that Atchison, while supervising the annual audits of Lincoln, had written several letters to banking regulators and United States senators vigorously supporting the aggressive lending and investment practices of Keating and Lincoln.

> Atchison seemed to drop the auditor's traditional stance of independence by repeatedly defending the practices of Lincoln and its corporate parent to Congress and federal regulators . . . Since when does the outside accountant—the public watchdog—become a proponent of the client's affairs? [3]

During the summer of 1988, the relationship between officers of Lincoln and the audit engagement partner who replaced Atchison, Janice Vincent, began to deteriorate. Vincent testified that disagreements arose with Lincoln management during the summer of 1988

---

3. E.N. Berg, "The Lapses by Lincoln's Auditors," *New York Times* (December 28, 1989): D6.

over the proper accounting treatment for several of the savings and loan's large real estate transactions. The most serious disagreement stemmed from a proposed exchange of assets between Lincoln and another corporation which would have resulted in a $50 million "paper" profit for Lincoln. Charles Keating was very upset when Vincent steadfastly maintained that the $50 million profit should not be recorded in Lincoln's accounting records. Following additional confrontations with Vincent regarding the propriety of the accounting treatment applied to other large transactions of Lincoln, Keating requested a meeting with Vincent and the managing partner of Arthur Young. At one point during that meeting, Keating turned to Vincent and remarked, "Lady, you have just lost a job." [4] In fact, the managing partner of Arthur Young sided with Vincent and subsequently informed Keating that Arthur Young was resigning as the auditor of both ACC and Lincoln Savings and Loan.

Act III

At 7:05 P.M. on July 5, 1982, a squad of bank examiners from the FDIC locked the doors of the Penn Square Bank of Oklahoma City, Oklahoma. Thus ended the legacy of a small shopping center bank that grew from total assets of $29 million in 1974 when it was acquired by B.P. "Beep" Jennings, an Oklahoma oilman and banker, to total assets of more

---

4. Committee on Banking, Finance and Urban Affairs, House of Representatives. *Investigation of Lincoln Savings and Loan Association, Part 4* (Washington, D.C.: U.S. Government Printing Office, 1990).

than $500 million at the time of its closing. The more than $1.5 billion in losses suffered by Penn Square, its affiliated banks, uninsured depositors, and the FDIC insurance fund made this bank failure the most costly in United States history at the time.

The deluge of lawsuits subsequent to the closing of Penn Square ensnared a wide range of parties, including the bank's audit firm, Peat, Marwick, Mitchell & Company. Peat Marwick became an easy target of third parties who were attempting to assign the burden of responsibility for the bank's collapse. Particularly critical of Peat Marwick was Representative Fernand St Germain, chairman of the congressional committee that investigated the collapse of Penn Square. At one point during the congressional hearings, a Peat Marwick partner explained that his firm's audit opinion was intended only for the bank's directors, implying that external parties had not relied on the unqualified opinion that Peat Marwick issued on Penn Square's 1981 financial statements three months prior to the bank's closing. The partner's caveat provoked an indignant response from Representative St Germain.

> You are not aware of the fact that the people at Penn Square dealing with brokers gave your reports . . . to people, credit unions, S&Ls around this nation who put enormous sums of money into this institution based on your audit reports, since that was all that was available . . . Did it come as a complete and total surprise to you, like the fact that when you get to be 10 years old you find out that there is no Santa Claus? [5]

---

5. Committee on Banking, Finance and Urban Affairs, House of Representatives. *Penn Square Bank Failure* (Washington, D.C.: U.S. Government Printing Office, 1982).

The Oklahoma City office of the accounting firm of Arthur Young & Company audited Penn Square's annual financial statements from 1976 through 1980. For the years ending December 31, 1976, through December 31, 1979, the bank received unqualified audit opinions from Arthur Young. However, in 1980, Arthur Young issued a qualified opinion on Penn Square's financial statements, an opinion which disclosed that the audit firm had concerns regarding the adequacy of the bank's loan loss reserve. Harold Russell, the managing partner of the Oklahoma City office of Arthur Young, subsequently testified that Jennings was "not pleased" with the audit firm's decision to qualify the 1980 opinion. Without prior warning, Jennings informed Russell in late November 1981 that the bank had decided to retain the accounting firm of Peat, Marwick, Mitchell & Company to audit its 1981 financial statements.

Representative St Germain's congressional investigative committee was very interested in determining why Peat Marwick was selected as the bank's audit firm following the dismissal of Arthur Young. Jim Blanton, the managing partner of Peat Marwick's Oklahoma City office, informed the committee that several members of his firm were well acquainted with top executives of Penn Square prior to his firm being selected as the bank's new auditor. Blanton suggested that these relationships were responsible, at least in part, for Penn Square's decision to retain Peat Marwick as its new audit firm in the fall of 1981.

Under further questioning by members of the congressional committee, Blanton disclosed that a number of Peat Marwick's Oklahoma City partners had previously obtained more than $2 million in loans and a $1 million line of credit from Penn Square.

These loans presented the audit firm with an independence "problem" that had to be resolved before the bank could be accepted as a client. The agreement reached between the two parties was that Penn Square would sell the loans and the line of credit to other banks. In spite of this understanding, on July 1, 1982—just four days prior to the bank's closing—Peat Marwick learned that one of the loans had been repurchased by Penn Square. A Peat Marwick official testified during the congressional hearings that this repurchase had been done without his firm's knowledge and that it was "completely contrary to our prior understanding with the bank." [6]

QUESTIONS

1. Define, in your own words, the meaning of the phrase "professional ethics."

2. How should a profession determine what constitutes "ethical" behavior?

3. What were Jose Gomez's ethical responsibilities when he was informed by Alan Novick of the material undisclosed errors in the 1977 and 1978 financial statements of ESM Government Securities, Inc.?

4. Identify the parties who were affected by Gomez's decision not to disclose those errors and indicate how these parties were affected.

5. Prior to the completion of the 1987 Lincoln audit, Charles Keating approached Jack Atchison regarding

---

6. Ibid.

the possibility of Atchison accepting a job with ACC. Comment on whether or not you believe this situation likely affected the independence of Atchison given that he was supervising the 1987 Lincoln audit at the time.

6. Several partners in the Oklahoma City office of Peat Marwick obtained loans from Penn Square Bank prior to the date the bank became an audit client. Assuming that no additional loans were made by Penn Square Bank to Peat Marwick personnel after the bank became an audit client and that none of the members of the Penn Square audit team had received loans from the bank, why did these earlier loans present an independence problem to Peat Marwick?

7. Assume that in August 1979 Jose Gomez had decided to inform the national managing partner of Alexander Grant that the 1977 and 1978 financial statements of ESM contained material errors that were not detected by the audits supervised by Gomez. Draft a memo by Gomez to the national managing partner in which he makes this revelation. In the memo, indicate how you, in the role of Gomez, would have suggested that the situation be handled. Assume the following additional facts in preparing your memo: 1) The fraud was skillfully concealed by ESM personnel from Gomez and his subordinates, 2) Gomez believed that ESM would be forced out of business if the errors were revealed, 3) if the errors were not revealed, Gomez believed that ESM would likely recoup the losses in the following twelve months, and 4) if the errors were revealed and ESM was forced out of business, Alexander Grant would likely be sued successfully by the customers and creditors of ESM.

INDEX